Transport, the Environment and Economic Policy

Transport, the Environment and Economic Policy

Kenneth Button

Professor of Applied Economics and Transport
Loughborough University,
and
VSB Visiting Professor of Transport and the Environment
Tinbergen Institute, Free University of Amsterdam

Edward Elgar

Published by
Edward Elgar Publishing Limited
Gower House
Croft Road
Aldershot
Hants GU11 3HR

Edward Elgar Publishing Company
Old Post Road
Brookfield
Vermont 05036
USA

A CIP catalogue record for this book is available from the British Library

A CIP catalogue record for this book is available from the US Library of Congress

Reprinted 1995

ISBN 1 85278 443 1

Printed and bound in Great Britain by
Ipswich Book Co. Ltd., Ipswich, Suffolk

Contents

Figures

Tables

Preface

The motivation for writing this short book stems from an interest in the application of economic ideas to the problems posed by transport to the environment. My personal interest in transport and environmental issues stems back nearly twenty years but was particularly focused during the early 1990s when I was working for the Organisation for Economic Cooperation and Development examining matters such as the causes of excessive adverse impacts of transport on the environment, the potential use of economic instruments to ameliorate them and the problems of integrating environmental factors with traditional economic considerations in policy formulation. The work has been further stimulated during a period as VSB Visiting Professor in Transport and the Environment at the Tinbergen Institute in the Netherlands. The VSB Foundation's assistance allowed me both time to gather further data for the work and the opportunity to produce the final manuscript.

Listening to Desert Island Discs, marooned authors often seem to claim that, since it is a lonely experience writing a book, isolation holds few fears for them. In fact, it seems to me that it is the family of those who insist on producing books who must suffer from the greatest loneliness as the selfish writer, at best, ignores them when things go well and, at worst, blames them when things go badly. So finally, I must thank my wife, Elizabeth, and two children, Alexandra and James, for bearing with me while I battled with my Powerbook to produce this book. I am sure I could never be as tolerant as they are!

Kenneth Button

1   Introduction

1.1   Background

Transport forms an important part of everyone's life. Adequate transport is something that we all tend to take for granted in the industrialised world and if it is not available public outcries soon emerge. The reasons for this are not difficult to find. Comprehensive transport provision is perceived as an important input into the efficient functioning of modern industry and commerce. It also affords individuals and households the benefits of mobility and access.

From the production perspective it fosters, for example, the development of more cohesive markets and permits greater exploitation of economies of scale, scope and density in the production process. Modern management techniques such as 'just-in-time' practices would not be possible without fast and, perhaps what is more important, reliable transport. There would be little point in moving towards a Single European Market (or an even wider 'European Economic Space') if there was not a comprehensive and modern European transport system, although the exact scale and nature of such a system is open to debate. More generally, the global specialisation of production that is gradually emerging as industry seeks to exploit each country's comparative advantage in production would not be possible without modern transport and communications systems.

At the personal level, transport affords individuals wider employment choice and, as economic development progresses and people have more leisure opportunities, so the recreational and social options that are available to them are increased. It also serves an important political function in helping both to cause spatial political integration and to link disparate geographical groups into the mainstream of decision making.

From an environmental perspective, transport has also conferred considerable benefits. The horse- and oxen-drawn economies of the past may have allowed the attainment of some form of eco-balance, but without motorised transport urban areas had to be geographically concentrated, with the resultant adverse implications that this implied for health and the general quality of city life. Even the arrival of rail transport, which was important in the wider industrial revolutions of the eighteenth and nineteenth centuries, did not resolve the problems of urban distribution systems. Indeed, by concentrating inter-urban consignments and deliveries at rail hubs it made them worse in many instances.

Against these undoubted advantages which modern transport and its associated enhanced mobility have brought to society it has linked with it very serious economic costs. Historically, transport has been seen as generating significant environmental problems as well as benefits. There is plenty of evidence from antiquity, for instance, of cities banning horse-drawn transport during certain hours and requiring users of draught animals to clean up after their passage. In the past, transport, in another sense, imposed many unappreciated environmental costs of which the most serious was, perhaps, the spread of disease. It facilitated, for example, the spread of the Black Death in traded wool products and the taking of Old World diseases to the Americas and Australasia after the voyages of discovery, for example, by Columbus and Tasman.

While many other economic activities impact on the environment, modern transport, in part because of its scale and visibility, has been the subject of specific concern amongst those interested in the environment. This concern has been expressed as much by economists as by other groups. Scanning through the academic literature in economics, for instance, we find:

- Surface transport described by Thomson (1974) as,

> ... an engineering industry carried on, not privately within the walls of a factory, but in public places where people are living, working, shopping and going about their daily business. The noise, smell, danger and other unpleasant features of large, fast-moving machinery are brought close to people, with potentially devastating consequences for the human environment.

- Baumol and Oates (1979) in their seminal work on environmental economics state that,

> ...some of the most pervasive externalities are generated not by industrial operations, but by individual activities. The automobile is a notorious producer of detrimental spillovers. Automobile exhausts increase laundry expenses, make it more difficult to breathe, and even shorten lives. The heavy cloud of pollutants that hangs over crowded roadways, the widespread traffic delays, and the heavy accident rates in such areas again suggest that externalities created by the activities of consumers are not the exceptional phenomena.

- Mishan (1967) looking at the welfare economics problems of modern urban areas discovers that,

> Hoarse beneath the fumes emitted by the endless swarm of crawling vehicles, today's city bears close resemblance to some gigantic and clamorous arsenal.

1.2   The Economist's Interest in the Environment

Much of the recent debate on environmental matters has tended to push the importance of economics to one side. Many ecology groups, in particular, combine political ideology with environmental activism in which trade-offs of any kind are deemed impossible. Indeed, one could well be led to believe that economists have never had much interest in environmental matters and have been dragged into recent debates on the subject, of which the transport element is but one component, only rather reluctantly.

The facts, though, are rather different and, indeed, professional economists and those with an interest in economic matters have long been concerned with the state of the environment. One must admit, however, that a strong tie between transport studies and environmental economics is comparatively recent.

One of the most cited (and, one suspects, least read) books relating to this area of economics is Pigou's (1920) *The Economics of Welfare*. This provides the analytical basis upon which much modern economic thinking on environmental policy is based. Even before this, however, such classical economists as Malthus and Ricardo were concerned in the early nineteenth century with the long-term prospects of declining living standards due to the scarcity of good quality agricultural land and natural resources more generally. While much of this nineteenth century work was theoretical in orientation and supported, in the main, by anecdotal illustrations, Stanley Jevons' pessimistic conclusions drawn from statistical analysis of coal depletion rates, although flawed, provided an early illustration of concern over the running down of non-renewable resource stocks.

The concern with the depletion of non-renewable resources was supplemented in neo-classical economics, to which Pigou's work belongs, by the notion that there may exist market failures. In normal circumstances a perfectly functioning market would optimise resource allocation, including the rate of depletion of non-renewable resources, and maximise social welfare - the Pareto optimal situation.

In practice, however, there may be circumstances when the market fails to achieve this and it is in these circumstances that government action is required. Lack of markets in environmental 'goods' is an obvious example of such a failure but much of the attention of the early neo-classical economists prior to Pigou was directed towards such things as monopoly power and indivisibilities in demand and supply. In transport, for instance, such questions as second-best pricing, peak-load pricing, joint costs and market instability dominated the market failures considered when rail was the dominant mode.

Pigou's work helped highlight the need to bring environmental costs and benefits into the economic calculus, but besides being of academic interest its actual impact on policy formulation in transport or other spheres was, in retrospect, rather limited. This is equally true of the initial impact of the work of Coase (1960) which sought explicitly to deal with the issues of property rights and transactions costs. He argued strongly that many environmental problems could be efficiently resolved by allocating either rights to a clean environment or rights to pollute (it made no difference in the long term which) and then allowing individuals to trade these rights. He recognised, however, the imperfections of the market and appreciated that the costs of finding trading partners and negotiating and enforcing prices would be impracticable in many cases. His work, has, however, led more recently to some innovative policy actions (e.g. marketable permits) which have relevance to transport.

The increased concern with rather more macro-environmental issues, and most especially matters such as global warming, biodiversity, ozone depletion, and so on which grew in the 1960s, particularly in the context of natural resource depletion, also drew in a considerable number of economists. In particular, Boulding's (1966) work both resurrected interest in economics' importance when considering environmental matters and brought a wider perspective to the debate. Essentially, he saw the Earth as a spaceship that could draw energy from the Sun and finite fossil fuel reserves, but was reliant on the recycling of water and the growing of its own food. The conclusion of such an approach is that it may not be possible in the future to continue to enjoy economic growth. This type of approach led the way to notions of 'sustainable development'.

The notion of 'sustainable development' came to the forefront of many debates in the 1980s. The exact definition has subsequently and regularly been redefined and rethought through a variety of studies and reports. *Blueprint for a Green Economy* (Pearce *et al*, 1989), which has proved very influential in shaping thinking about approaches to sustainable development in the UK, devotes an entire chapter to questions of definition. The Organisation for Economic Cooperation and Development in Paris, in a review of the definitions which have been used, came up in 1989 with no fewer than 64 distinct notions of what sustainable development implies and the list has grown considerably since that time. Perhaps the most helpful view is that expressed in the highly influential Brundtland Report (World Commission on Environment and Development, 1987);

> In essence, sustainable development is a process of change in which the exploitation of resources, the direction of investments, the orientation of technological development and institutional changes are all in harmony and enhance both current and future potential to meet human needs and aspirations.

More recently, economists have, therefore, become rather more involved in the environmental debate at an actual policy formulation level. It is interesting to speculate why this is so. In part it must stem from the improved techniques which economists have developed to handle environmental issues. More pragmatically, perhaps, it is rather more that policies based upon administrative or control systems have failed to produce the socially desired impact. In particular, regulation and control measures have been widely used but have often proved rather blunt and inflexible instruments. The quest for more efficient instruments has, almost by default, brought economists into many environmental debates, including those with a significant transport content. One should add to this that there is an increased awareness that environmental protection can lead to reduced economic growth in the narrow sense of GDP increases. Economic techniques have increasingly been deployed at both the micro- (e.g. in cost-benefit analysis) and macro-level (e.g. in 'Green Accounting') to highlight the trade-offs which this implies.

How influential the views of economists have been in the environmental debate both generally and more specifically regarding transport is unclear. It does seem, however, that rather more notice is now being taken of economic concepts and there is increasing interest in the use of economic instruments as a means for achieving environmental objectives. One can cite, for instance, the Council of the Organisation for Economic Cooperation and Development (1991a) which has argued for countries to 'make a greater and more consistent use of economic instruments' for environmental management. Equally, in their 5th Environmental Action Programme 1993-2000, the Commission of the European Communities (1992a) emphasises the important role which pollution charges can play generally while its Green Paper, *A Community Strategy for 'Sustainable Mobility'* (Commission of the European Communities, 1992b), highlights the importance of charges as part of a wider package of transport measures.

1.3 The Book

This book is not intended to be comprehensive in its coverage of the debates surrounding the appropriate policy stance to take regarding transport and the environment. It is written very much from the perspective of an economist and attempts to set down some of the main economic contributions to the on-going debates in this area. Equally, though, from the point of view of modern economics analysis, the book is decidedly non-mathematical, although a large number of diagrams are used to help in the exposition, and has the deliberate aim of being relatively accessible to anyone who has some basic training in the rudimentary elements of the subject. Indeed, it is hoped that people without even this background should not find the volume to daunting. Having said that, economics has become increasingly technical over the years and much of the original material that underlies the arguments in this book derives from articles and books containing a substantial amount of mathematics. For those interested in the finer points of the technical debates the book is comprehensively referenced.

The book, therefore, basically sets out to examine both the underlying economic theories that help us to understand the forces that lead to transport imposing excessively on the environment and to review the policy options open to tackle the resultant problems. It is a book primarily about economics; it is not strictly a book about ecology although the two are not easily separated. Because it is about economics the focus is inevitably on optimisation and, as a consequence, very much seeks to define guidelines that balance the needs of environmental protection against the other needs of society.

It is never easy to decide on the structure of a book and whatever format is selected inevitably has problems associated with it. In this case the structure seeks to offer some basic background to the transport sector, some idea of the scale and costs of the environmental intrusion that it imposes and some discussion of various aspects of policy. This seems to offer a way into the topic for those unfamiliar with the details of transport provision and use. It also fits in broadly with the way in which transport-related topics are generally addressed. Alternatively one could have adopted a problem-based approach and looked specifically at particular types of environmental issue (e.g. local transport-induced environmental problems such as noise or global issues such as the contribution of transport to greenhouse gas levels) or an approach in terms of the contribution of different modes of transport to the current environmental situation. The former, however, would inevitably have led to considerable overlap in the discussion of underlying economic issues while the latter would have disguised many points that transcend individual modal consideration.

The early chapters (Chapters 2 and 3) of the book look at the setting in which we are operating. They provide details of the nature of the transport systems that exist and the forms of policy that are used to govern them. Since the World is not static, they also look at some of the trends that are going to be important in the longer-term development of transport. As far as possible the account is international but there is an inevitable bias towards the situation in the industrialised countries of the world. This focus can be justified both in terms of the information available and by the fact that it is these countries which in general have the largest transport systems. The developing world and post-communist states of Eastern Europe are not, however, entirely ignored. They are places where future growth in transport demand can be anticipated. The scale and forms of environmental intrusion imposed by transport are set against this background.

Some space (Chapter 4) is devoted to reviewing just how much we know about the monetary costs of the physical environmental impacts of transport. A review of the techniques of evaluation is presented together with a details of some of the values which have been produced and are used, in some countries, for decision making. What emerges is that, while it is clear that our knowledge in this area is far from complete, there is still a substantial body of work which can help in making important policy trade-offs on a consistent monetary bias.

This is followed by an examination of the relevant welfare economic theory which underlies much of our understanding of the root causes of the current concern that exists for the environment - and as we have seen, contrary to many commonly-held views, economists have long been interested in issues concerning environmental degradation and excessive natural resource depletion.

Chapters 5 and 6 continue with this general theme but, while Chapter 5 focuses on rather traditional views of the environmental problems created by failures of market mechanisms, Chapter 6 looks at the problems created when either misguided, or simply ill-thought-out, government transport policies lead to environmental problems or the worsening of existing problems - the so-called problem of intervention failures. This effectively extends the traditional neo-classical set of ideas of externalities that have long held sway in economics to embrace the ideas of the Public Choice School.

The latter part of the book is concerned directly with policy responses to the environmental problems thrown up by transport. The portfolio of tools available to the authorities and their uses are examined. These instruments naturally include a variety of economic or 'fiscal' tools such as emission charges, taxation reform, road pricing and parking fees (examined in Chapter 7) but, accepting that there may be circumstances where their application is not appropriate or economically efficient, a range of other regulatory approaches embracing such things as standards, land-use planning and moral suasion are also discussed (Chapter 8).

The final chapter looks, albeit rather briefly, at the political economy of environmental policy in the context of the transport sector. It considers, for instance, issues of international co-ordination of policy and the reasons why particular policy instruments tend to be favoured by policy makers. The chapter is essentially general in its coverage but there is also some brief discussion of the economic problems involved in reaching agreement on environmental policies at the international level.

2 The Transport System and Transport Policy

2.1 Introduction

To appreciate the environmental implications of transport and to gain some understanding of the options open to policy makers, and also the types of constraint confronting them, it is helpful to examine some of the details of the transport market itself. The aim of this brief chapter, therefore, is to summarise some of the basic features of modern transport and to outline the natures of the institutional systems that have been developed to handle policy issues.

The chapter attempts to look at the overall transport picture but there are limitations to this. In particular, transport is not a homogeneous product. Clearly there are distinctions between freight and passenger transport but heterogeneity extends well beyond this. International, domestic and local transport is another oft-used categorisation but again this misses many important distinctions that exist. Essentially, each route and service is a unique product reflecting a variety of individual spatial and temporal characteristics as well as a diversity of qualitative aspects (e.g. safety, comfort, reliability, capacity, etc.). Thus while here, and to some extent in the following chapters, we tend to set out general patterns and data about transport and the environment, the micro-implications, which are obviously often extremely important for individuals, can vary considerably for specific transport services from the generalisations presented here. Aggregation, which is essential for defining issues and discussing broad policy options, cannot be avoided but local variations exist and can often prove to be important.

2.2 The Scale of the Sector

Transport is an integral part of any modern economy. It provides a vital input into manufacturing processes (indeed, some 1,295 thousand million tonne-kilometres of freight transport were done during 1987 in European Conference of Ministers of Transport countries) and permits society to enjoy a wide range of geographically disparate, leisure activities. Transport use has grown, with economic expansion being both a creative impetus to the economic development process and a consequence of it. Transport shapes urban form and is influential in determining the spatial distribution of economic activities (e.g. see papers in Button and Gillingwater, 1986).

The importance of transport in the wider economy and in macro-economic policy making becomes apparent when it is realised that transport supply industries contribute 7 percent directly to the Gross Domestic Product of the European Economic Community with further, far-reaching, secondary links through personal consumption of transport services. The share of the private consumption budget devoted to transport and communication in North America has risen from 14.9 percent in 1960 to 16.3 percent in 1983 and is forecast to rise to 18.6 percent by the year 2000 (United Nations Economic Commission for Europe, 1987). The same source projects a 16.7 percent share of the European Community's market budget going to transport by the year 2000 from a base of 14.5 percent in 1983.

Transport expenditure also extends beyond the simple financial window. From a different perspective, for instance, at the personal level it has been estimated that travel accounts for one hour per individual per day in developed economies (Zahavi, 1979).

The 'hardware' required to meet this level of transport use has resulted in the growth of substantial automobile, aircraft and ship-building industries and the maintenance of massive civil engineering construction activities. In the US, automobile production, for example, accounts for some 12 percent of the country's aluminium consumption, 19 percent of steel consumption, 20 percent of machine tools manufactured, 50 percent of the lead produced and 67 percent of its rubber output.

This in turn results in large-scale employment in transport-related industries - in the pre-unified FRG, for example, some 1.8 million jobs (7 percent of the labour force) are dependent on the demand for and use of motor cars and in the US some 20 percent of the labour force in 1980 was in jobs directly or indirectly related to automobile production. In the Netherlands some 13 percent of the total employment is related to transport.

Transport is also a major source of government revenue in many countries with fuel taxes representing 6.8 percent of the Irish Republic's government revenue in 1983, 5.5 percent of Italy's, 4.7 percent of the UK's and 3.9 percent on average across the European Community states. In total, road taxes amounted to some 6.2 percent of the Netherlands' government revenue in 1982-84, 8.6 percent of New Zealand's, 3.4 percent of Japan's, 7.8 percent of Switzerland's, 7.0 percent of Australia's and 6.3 percent of Sweden's.

While there has been increased use made of virtually all modes of transport within Organisation for Economic Cooperation and Development states (for instance, freight transport grew, in tonne-kilometres, by 39.6 percent between 1970 and 1986 and passenger movements, in passenger-kilometres, by 59.2 percent), albeit to differ-

ent degrees within individual members, quantitatively it has been
land-based transport (and motor vehicles in particular) which have
witnessed the greatest increase in usage. The number of both cars and
goods vehicles have increased significantly in recent years. There has
been a corresponding increase in traffic volumes. For example,
between 1970 and 1987 car traffic, measured in vehicle-kilometres, rose
by 79 percent in France, 85 percent in Italy, 49 percent in the US, 82
percent in the UK and 77 percent in the FRG. Equally, goods
movements by road have increased substantially; again between 1970
and 1987 vehicle-kilometres have risen by 93 percent in France, 93 percent in Italy, 49 percent in the US, 45 percent in the UK and 34 percent
in the old FRG.

Table 2.1
Transport infrastructure in selected OECD countries (1986)

Country	Roads (motorways) thousand kilometres	Rail (electrified) thousand kilometres
Austria	12(1.2)	5.1(3.0)
Belgium	16(1.5)	3.7(2.0)
Denmark	70(0.6)	2.5(0.2)
Federal Republic of Germany	490(8.2)	31.0(12.0)
Finland	76(0.2)	5.9(1.5)
France	800(6.0)	35.0(11.0)
Greece	110(0.1)	2.5(-)
Irish Republic	92(0.1)	1.9(-)
Italy	300(5.9)	20.0(10.0)
Japan	1,100(3.6)	n.a.
Netherlands	97(2.0)	2.8(1.8)
Norway	86(0.3)	4.2(2.4)
Portugal	50(0.2)	3.6(0.5)
Spain	220(2.1)	14.0(6.4)
Sweden	130(1.4)	12.0(7.5)
Switzerland	70(1.1)	5.1(5.1)
UK	370(2.9)	17.0(3.8)
USA	6,300(960.0)	240.0(1.7)
Yugoslavia	140(0.7)	9.3(3.5)

Source: Organisation for Economic Cooperation and Development (1988b)

This increased use of land-based transport has necessitated (and
been facilitated by) the provision of extensive infrastructure. The
amount of road, rail, port and airport capacity in most OECD member
states is now considerable (see Table 2.1 for some selected data) and is
expanding. The Congress of the US, for example, voted for $254 billion
of investment in transport infrastructure between 1988 and 1992.
Indeed, investment in such infrastructure often represents a not
insignificant component of many countrie's national income (see
Table 2.2). In broad terms, recent years have seen a reduction in
investment in new transport infrastructure but more resources being
expended on maintenance. Indeed, the total length of rail network in

OECD countries declined by 4.1 percent between 1970 and 1985 although the proportion of electrified lines rose from 29.3 percent to 38.6 percent. Future infrastructure plans for Europe, both on an EC basis and for individual countries (see Button, 1990a), suggest that there may, however, be something of an upsurge in investment in transport infrastructure expenditure into the next century, especially in terms of major, high-speed rail projects.

Table 2.2
Transport infrastructure investment in selected EC countries (1982-5)

| Country | Infrastructure investment as % of GDP | |
	Road	Rail
Belgium	0.67	0.29
France	0.65	0.09
Germany	0.79	0.26
Italy	0.62	0.27
Spain	0.50	0.27
United Kingdom	0.40	0.09

Source: European Conference of Ministers of Transport (1988)

This investment in transport combined with the nature of local geography and trade patterns affects the overall mobility that any country enjoys. Exact measurement of mobility is not easy but some indication of the mobility levels enjoyed on a per capita basis by both passengers and freight traffic over a range of countries is set out in Table 2.3. While one may doubt the exact meaning of the composite measure adopted (involving the combining of such things as passenger miles per annum of automobile, rail and domestic air travel; miles of railway; ton-miles of railway freight; miles of road and number of lorries) the broad impression is probably accurate. The scale and nature of the transport systems do differ significantly across countries with marked divergence between the conditions in the industrial states and Third World countries. The importance of this for the environment, in both the short term (in the context of the nature of development processes on the environment) and the longer term (as more countries become industrialised and their transport use increases), is an issue considered below.

2.3   The Transport Mix

Countries vary both in the aggregate use that they make of transport and their provision of transport facilities and in the particular forms of transport which are favoured. There are obvious financial and physical constraints confronting many users of transport, especially in Third World countries but, even accepting this, the vast majority of individuals have a choice of mode in which to undertake their travel and consignors have a variety of modes in which they can send their goods. Looking at developments over recent years anumber of very clear patterns emerge both in terms of passenger and freight transport.

Table 2.3
Index of per capita GNP and mobility (France=100)

	GNP per capita	Travel mobility	Freight mobility
Switzerland	139	104	81
Sweden	119	96	151
Germany	117	101	57
Belgium	109	88	117
Norway	106	55	107
USA	106	160	260
Netherlands	101	83	42
France	100	100	100
Canada	95	114	374
Australia	91	107	335
Japan	87	96	94
UK	63	78	47
Czechoslovakia	53	54	132
Italy	53	86	49
Spain	43	54	44
USSR	40	34	229
Hungary	38	34	68
Venezuela	31	24	36
Yugoslavia	24	32	55
Argentina	24	32	114
Iran	22	10	10
Brazil	18	18	23
Mexico	15	14	42
Korea	15	8	16
Malaysia	14	11	26
Turkey	14	5	26
Ecuador	11	5	21
Colombia	11	6	47
Nigeria	6	5	5
Philippines	6	2	18
Egypt	5	5	13
Indonesia	3	3	5
Pakistan	2	3	10
China	2	3	16
India	2	5	26
Ethiopia	1	2	3
Bangladesh	1	2	3

Source: Owen (1987)

What determines this pattern is a topic of considerable interest but any detailed consideration is beyond the scope of this volume. The importance of this choice, in our context, is that different forms of transport, as we see in later chapters, affect the environment in different ways.

In terms of hard numbers, Table 2.4 offers aggregate data on the choices actually made regarding freight transport mode in the major industrialised and some former communist countries. It excludes air freight although this is a significant mode, and one growing in importance, concerning the movement of mail and small consignments. It also misses out marine shipping which is obviously the dominant mode for international bulk movements in many parts of the world.

Table 2.4
Mode split for freight in selected European countries (thousand /tonnes/ kms in 1988)

Country	Road	Rail	Inland waterways
European Community			
Belgium	26.00	7.00	6.35
Denmark	9.10	1.66	....
France	111.80	52.30	7.33
Germany	15.40	58.50	52.80
Greece	14.00	0.60	....
Ireland	5.00	0.55	....
Italy	169.00	19.60	0.14
Luxembourg	0.40	0.64	0.36
Netherlands	22.10	3.20	33.85
Portugal	9.00	1.56	....
Spain	133.00	12.00	....
United Kingdom	124.00	18.20	2.30
Eastern Europe			
Bulgaria	14.70	17.60	....
Czechoslovakia	13.10	69.40	5.20
GDR	16.40	59.40	2.50
Hungary	3.20	20.20	2.00
Poland	38.80	120.70	1.40
Yugoslavia	20.90*	25.40	4.60

* Public transport only
Source: Taken from United Nations, European Conference of Ministers of Transport, International Road Federation and International Union of Railways data sets.

Table 2.5 sets down choices of passenger mode, this time in the context of the main EC Member States. Inclusion of US data would show a much greater use of automobiles and a significant number of domestic air passenger-miles - bus and rail passenger miles are substantially lower. Again the data is not complete and excludes both walking and cycling trips that, in many urban situations and in a large number of Third World countries, represent the main means of personal transport. The main excuse for excluding walking and cycling is the dearth of reliable aggregate data on the topic.

The importance of road transport for both person and freight movement is clear and the trend is for the dominance of the mode, other things being equal, to increase rather than diminish in the fu-

ture. This is particularly likely if the post-communist countries of
Eastern Europe expand their economies by turning to manufacturing
and modern methods of management, as many commentators anticipate for the early part of the next century. These developments, if the
patterns of the West are mirrored, will favour the attributes of speed,
door-to-door service and more direct control offered by road transport
but equally this will have significant environmental implications.

Table 2.5
Trends in European passenger traffic (billion passengers)

	1970	1975	1980	1984	1985	1986
Private cars	1306.9	1542.3	1828.0	1972.0	2005.7	2109.4
France	304.7	374.8	452.5	491.7	494.4	517.3
Germany	350.6	405.4	470.3	483.1	481.6	510.3
Belgium	49.2	57.5	65.4	67.8	67.4	68.1
Italy	230.0	279.3	324.0	355.3	373.7	394.4
United Kingdom	267.0	294.0	365.0	410.3	424.8	448.0
Netherlands	72.1	93.5	112.5	122.8	120.8	126.2
Denmark	33.3	37.8	38.3	41.1	43.0	45.1
Rail	66.3	179.9	192.8	196.7	196.0	200.1
France	47.1	57.2	62.2	69.1	71.2	68.4
Germany	37.3	36.9	40.5	39.0	37.4	40.5
Belgium	7.6	7.5	7.0	6.4	6.6	6.5
Italy	32.5	36.3	39.6	39.1	37,4	40.5
United Kingdom	30.4	30.3	30.3	29.7	29.7	30.8
Netherlands	8.0	8.5	8.9	9.0	9.2	8.9
Denmark	3.4	3.2	4.3	4.4	4.5	8.1
Bus and coach	187.5	203.1	234.4	238.9	236.0	240.0
France	25.2	28.9	38.0	40.3	38.4	39.0
Germany	58.4	67.7	73.9	70.5	65.0	64.6
Belgium	3.0	3.2	3.1	2.9	3.1	3.0
Italy	37.4	42.3	57.8	63.0	66.6	70.6
United Kingdom	49.0	45.0	42.0	42.0	42.0	41.8
Netherlands	9.9	10.3	12.2	11.8	12.2	12.1
Denmark	4.6	5.7	7.4	8.4	8.7	8.9

The transport mix is obviously of general importance in environmental debates - for example, rail is often seen as more environmentally friendly than road transport - but this may be too simplistic since
one also has to consider input questions. An inefficient rail system, for
example, with large amounts of empty running and excess capacity
may prove less environmentally desirable than a road-based system
that is highly efficient and which exploits economies of density to the
full. Even within modes there are important differences, for instance,
at the national level. The inputs used for, say, a rail journey in Italy
may deviate considerably from those used in a similar journey in
France or the UK. By way of demonstration, Table 2.6 offers some

crude guidelines on differential rail productivity between a number of countries - rail being used here purely for illustrative purposes; it is expected that differences exist in all modes. The point here is that considerable variations in X-efficiency exist across transport systems and thus simple modal comparisons may well be misleading when attempting to define policies favouring a particular mode for environmental reasons.

Table 2.6
Rail productivity indicators

	Italy	UK	FRG	France
Employees	100	80	127	109
Network length	100	104	171	26
Employees per km of line	100	77	74	50
Travellers per km	100	76	102	147
Shipment (tonnes) per km	100	....	334	288
Productivity index of technical employees	100	146	176	193
Productivity index of blue collar employees	100	100	137	176

Source: Corriere della sera 31/8/88

There is a further dimension to the modal distribution. While the increased availability of land-based transport has brought unquestionable benefits to large sections of society its positive impact on enhancing the general level of accessibility has not been evenly spread and large numbers of individuals have found themselves relatively disadvantaged. Changes in the nature of land-based transport modes have contributed towards this. In particular, the widespread growth in car ownership in many countries during the post-Second World War period has been accompanied by a decline in the relative level of public transport provision. Studies of household travel behaviour (e.g. Hillman *et al*, 1976) suggest that this has had serious adverse implications for the mobility of those without easy access to an automobile. Equally, the arrival of motorised road-freight transport (the share of which, in tonne-kilometres, in ECMT member states rose from 49.1 percent in 1970 to 63.7 percent in 1987) has resulted in shifts in the relative commercial advantages enjoyed by different geographical regions to the economic detriment of some.

2.4 Financing Transport

Transport has to be financed and this involves a complicated set of actors. As we have seen above, the majority of passenger movements in industrialised countries are by automobile. The costs of part of these trips are borne by private individuals, but part is also borne by local or central government as providers of roads and other infrastructure. The complication here is that road users also pay for certain elements

of infrastructure (e.g. some river crossings and motorways) through
tolls (see Table 2.7). Additionally, there are taxes which are paid by
road users which are often implicitly treated as a user fee (e.g. annual
licence fees are seen as a sort of 'club' membership payment and fuel
tax as a sort of 'user' charge). As can be seen from Table 2.7 the relative
importance of such fees differs quite considerably between countries.

Table 2.7
Sources of revenue from road users in EC countries

Country	Percentage revenue from		
	Fuel tax	Vehicle tax	Tolls
Belgium	76	24	-
Denmark	62	38	-
Germany	75	25	-
Greece	83	17	-
France	74	12	14
Irish Republic	92	8	-
Italy	82	7	11
Luxemburg	86	14	-
Netherlands	59	41	-
Portugal	93	7	-
United Kingdom	71	29	-

Source: Organisation for Economic Cooperation and Development (1987)

In the case of rail, bus and air transport the user again pays in the
form of fares, but in many countries the authorities provide subsidies
that cover an element of either capital or operating costs. These subsidies and their implications for environmental policy are dealt with in
more detail in Chapter 6, but some indication of their importance for
urban public transport finance can be seen in the figures set out in
Table 2.8.

Linked with this is the issue of ownership. One of the important
changes in recent years is that there has been a tendency for increased
reliance on the private sector to finance transport investments. There
has also been a move towards greater private ownership of many
forms of public transport (e.g. in aviation, the bus sector, railways, etc.)
and for private finance to be employed by nationally-owned companies (e.g. to finance the French TVG system). These moves have taken
a variety of forms - see Button (1992a) - and have resulted in various
levels of residual public participation. The motivations for these
changes have been varied. In part they have formed an element of
macroeconomic policies to raise government revenue - the privatisation of British Airways in 1987 raised £892 million and of the British
Airports Authority the following year raised £1,200 million in current
prices. But also it has to do with efficiency and the need for fresh financial injections to develop new infrastructure and to modernise
systems.

Table 2.8
Urban public transport operating subsidies

	Type of operating subsidy	Revenue/cost ratio (%)	Regulatory system
Denmark	Network/route	55-56	Planned/franchised
Belgium	Network	30-40	Planned
Finland	Network	57-92	Planned
France	Network	53	Planned/franchised
Greece	Network	40-50	Planned
Ireland	Network	80-95	Planned
Israel	Network	66	Planned/franchised
Italy	Network	24-28	Planned
Netherlands	Network/route	28-40	Planned
Norway	Network/route	55-60	Planned/franchised
Portugal	Network/route	67	Planned/market
Spain	Network	70-90	Planned
Sweden	Network/route	39-48	Planned/franchised
Switzerland	Network	54-82	Planned
Turkey	Network		Planned
United Kingdom	Route		Market
West Germany	Network	54	Planned
Yugoslavia	Network		Planned

Source: Andersen (1992)

In addition to the trend away from public financing and the privatisation which has been occurring there has also been an expansion in international co-operation of infrastructure investment funding. The international development agencies, such as the World Bank, Inter-American Bank and Asian Development Bank have always put substantial sums into improving the transport of low-income countries - the World Bank allocates about 12 percent of its total budget to transport projects - and the European Bank for Reconstruction and Development is following a similar pattern concerning the former communist states. Further to this, however, the integration of European economies within the EC has resulted in major investments being funded through a centralised EC system. Some of the funds come through direct grants as part of programmes aimed at regional development but part also comes in the form of loans from the European Investment Bank (EIB). Some idea of the growth of the latter can be seen in Table 2.9 which compares the 1989 level of loans with those for the entire period 1982-89. A point of particular interest is the amount going to urban transport investment that, because of the greater concentration of pollutants in cities, is of particular relevance from an environmental perspective.

Table 2.9
Individual EIB loans in the transport sector going to urban transport

Country	1982-9		1989	
	Urban	Total	Urban	Total
Belgium	-	-	-	-
Denmark	-	696.3	-	282.2
Germany	31.4	157.7	26.5	114.0
Greece	-	395.4		31.8
Spain	31.0	747.8	9.2	340.4
France	106.9	2,155.5	106.9	607.0
Ireland	49.6	477.9	-	57.7
Italy	120.2	2,717.0	26.6	476.3
Luxembourg	-	18.0	-	-
Netherlands	-	257.5	-	172.5
Portugal	-	514.0	-	183.5
United Kingdom	-	1,381.7	-	305.7
Total	339.1	9518.6	169.2	2570.9

Methods of public financing differ markedly between countries. In many Third World nations, and in a number of the post-communist states, new investments in transport are often funded by international agencies such as the World Bank through grants and soft loans. National governments may contribute directly to a state's transport system but frequently, and especially regarding infrastructure of local importance and with respect to operations, the finance is through state or local (often urban) authorities. In most cases these lower tiers of government also have fiscal authority in their own right and can finance some degree of transport provision and can charge transport users independently of any central government control. There is no standard framework, however, which typifies this relationship between state and lower-tier government.

The importance of the financial arrangements surrounding transport provision and use is that many environmental problems stem from inappropriate or inadequate fiscal regimes. The nature and level of charges placed on transport suppliers and the mechanisms by which transport investment funds are allocated can influence both the scale of transport use and the form that this use can take.

2.5   The Policy-Making Institutions

In all countries of the world there exists a plethora of rules and regulations governing the operations of the transport sector. These rules cover a variety of overlapping geographical areas. It is helpful in understanding how environmental policy has developed regarding transport to consider just where the levels of responsibility lie and exactly what roles the different institutions play. In many cases the institutions have divergent interests and these can result in many of the intervention failures that are discussed in Chapter 6.

At the international level policy making essentially involves bargaining and co-operation. At the highest level, there are periodic meetings involving nation states, often held under the auspices of the United Nations or one of its agencies, which seek to reach agreement on tackling particular environmental issues. Almost by definition these are matters of global concern (e.g. fears of global warning or reduced biodiversity) which require co-ordinated action. The outcomes of such meetings are general agreements or the acceptance of guidelines to be followed by the states involved. It is usually left to individual countries to carry through the measures within their own legal framework and using appropriate instruments for their domestic circumstances. The economic dimension of such meetings usually comes in at the macro-level with countries, especially the economically less developed ones, seeking compensation for acting to protect the environment. The problems involved here are looked at in Chapter 9.

Additional to the periodic summit meetings there are a number of ongoing international committees that look at specific issues, e.g. the Law of the Seas. The issues here are often rather more down to earth and frequently involve the operationalising of the broader agreements reached at the summit meetings. There are also periodic, somewhat smaller meetings, which are aimed at tackling specific issues and come out with very firm policies, e.g. the Montreal Protocol on Substances that Deplete the Ozone Layer.

Of course, at these levels specific transport-related issues are hidden under the broader policy approaches which are being developed. Further down the decision-making tree, however, there is an increased tendency to begin to divide issues along sectoral lines. The European Community, for example, takes a broad policy approach to the environment within the Member States but also, as we saw in the previous chapter, then goes on to draw out conclusions and develop policies for individual sectors. It also has certain legal powers and agreements amongst members have been responsible for such things as the compulsory fitting of catalytic converters and for the soon-to-be initiated carbon taxes. It also has developed legal procedures for incorporating environmental factors into decision making, e.g. into decisions regarding transport infrastructure appraisal. Finally, through its ability to direct resources within the Community (e.g. through the regional Development Fund and European Investment Bank) it can directly influence at the margin the nature of new investments of 'Community interest'.

Other international agencies, such as the World Bank, and the European Bank for Reconstruction and Development, can influence transport through their ability to control financial resources for investment and for the maintenance of transport infrastructure. Generally they insist on some form of environmental impact study before funds are awarded.

There are a number of highly respected international organisations which, despite yielding little real legal power, exercise considerable moral suasion and pressure through research and discussion. The Organisation for Economic Cooperation and Development is an obvious example while the European Conference of Ministers of Transport (ECMT) serves a more specialised role within the transport field. These and the other international organisations have overlapping membership that often means that their influence is rather more than superficially defined legal powers would suggest.

At the national level there are usually several ministries which have overlapping responsibilities for transport and the environment. For example, in the United Kingdom the Department of the Environment has overall responsibilities for environmental matters but the Department of Transport has specific interests as has the energy ministry. Conflicts can easily arise either because the ministries pursue different objectives or because they pursue the same objectives but adopt different means. As an umbrella over all the spending ministries the finance ministry (the Treasury in the UK context) can influence the extent to which the ministries responsible for the environment, transport, etc. can commit public resources to environmental programmes.

Local administrations generally have limited legal powers in their own right, especially if one is thinking of federal governments or large urban authorities, but equally they have the responsibility to carry through national transport policies. In this latter context there is generally a degree of *de facto* flexibility as to the interpretation of centrally devolved enabling legislation. This can be particularly important in matters such as local traffic management, noise enforcement, safety measures, parking policy, etc. It offers some degree of local flexibility and autonomy.

3   The Environmental
       Effects of Transport

3.1   Introduction

Transport affects the environment in a variety of ways. Indeed, one of the particular difficulties in developing environmentally optimal policies for the transport sector is the diversity of these impacts (Button, 1990b). There are also issues concerning exactly what elements should be included in the umbrella of environmental effects.

Traffic congestion is often seen as an environmental effect but this is only so in an indirect way. The direct costs of traffic congestion (i.e. excessive travel times, wear and tear on vehicles, etc.) are external to those imposing them but they are costs borne within the transport community and are best treated as efficiency losses for those using transport services. In strict economic terms, these types of situations enter into the theory of clubs and the issues become those of deciding mechanisms for allowing club membership (i.e. basic access to the transport infrastructure) and club use (the allocation of infrastructure space to club members). Of course, traffic congestion also affects third parties in terms of fumes, noise, community severance, etc. and these should be seen as the actual environmental effects of traffic. Thus, while the literature on time costs of congestion is extensive, it is given little attention here. The concern is, therefore, much more with the natural environment.

To assess and evaluate the quantitative importance of these various impacts it is necessary to go through a number of stages. Not all are as simple as they might initially appear - as Quinet (1990; 1991) has pointed out, the idea of social cost is often open to numerous interpretations. First, it is necessary to examine the current and predicted nature of the transport market, in other words to examine trends in transport use.

Second, it is important to clarify exactly what elements of the environment, both natural and built, we are particularly concerned with. The impact land-based transport has on these then needs to be quantified. Third, once physical measures are obtained, an overall impression of the importance of these effects is required. While there are several ways one may attempt to reduce the wide range of environmental effects associated with transport to a common denominator, the use of a monetary scale has advantages. How one can perform such a standardisation process is a topic left for the following chapter.

3.2   The Physical Impact on the Environment

Transport impinges on the environment in a multiplicity of ways. While all transport has associated with it adverse environmental effects, land transport, in part because of its overall importance in virtually all economies but also because much of it tends to be conducted close to environmentally sensitive areas (e.g. residential areas), is generally seen as particularly intrusive. The modes of land transport cause a variety of forms of environmental damage and these are set out, in very general terms, in Table 3.1. The table should be treated as indicative rather than definitive in the sense that many of the local forms of environmental intrusion vary in their intensity according to the surroundings in which the transport activity is undertaken. This is less the case, however, with environmental implications of a global kind (e.g. the generation of gases that contribute to the 'greenhouse effect' - or 'ozone holes' - and to the incidence of 'acid rain').

Further, environmental effects extend beyond the simple use of transport to the implications of providing the vehicles and infrastructure. Road building, for example, is disruptive of the natural environment and requires large quantities of stone, aggregate and bitumen, the extraction of which generate their own negative environmental effects. From a French study (cited in Lamure, 1990), it is also clear that maintenance of infrastructure is a major consumer of energy - as much as 30 percent of the undiscounted total energy cost of road infrastructure, including construction and its use by vehicles, over a 25-year time horizon. Similar situations regarding environmental costs of construction and maintenance pertain concerning railways. Equally, automobile manufacturing plants, railway workshops and ship construction yards are unsightly and their products require huge quantities of raw materials and energy.

Excessive use of transport has, therefore, major backward multiplier linkages on the natural environment through the mechanical and civil engineering-based industries and further on back to the extractive industries.

In more detail, transport has both direct and indirect implications for the environment - the uncompensated social costs of transport activities. Any brief listing of these implications must, by its nature, be indicative rather than comprehensive. Equally, there are both long-term implications, associated with transport infrastructure provision, and short-term implications, associated with the use made of that infrastructure, which are often difficult to separate out. It is generally agreed, however, that the major direct effects are important and diverse - e.g. see: Bouladon (1979), Sharp and Jennings (1976), Foster (1974), Kanafani (1983), Organisation for Economic Cooperation

Table 3.1
The main impacts of land transport on the environment

Mode	Air	Water Resources	Land Resources	Solid Waste	Noise	Accident Risk	Other Impacts
Rail			Land taken for rights of way & terminals; derilection of obsolete facilities	Abandoned lines, equipment & rolling stock	Noise & vibration around terminals & along lines	Derailment or collision of freight carrying hazardous substances	Partition or destruction of neighbourhoods, farmland & wild life habitats
Road	Local (CO, HC, NOx, fuel additives such as lead & particulates) Global (CO_2, CFC)	Pollution of surface water & groundwater by surface run-off; modification of water systems by road building	Land taken for infrastructure; extraction of road building materials	Abandoned spoil tips & rubble from road works; road vehicles withdrawn from service; waste oil	Noise & vibration from cars, motorcycles & lorries in cities & along main roads	Deaths, injuries & property damage from accidents; risk from transport of hazardous substances; risk of structural failure in old or worn road facilities	Partition or destruction of neighbourhoods, farmland & wild life habitats; congestion
Air	Air Pollution	Modification of water tables, river courses, & field drainage in airport construction	Land taken for infrastructure; dereliction of obsolete sites	Scrapped aircraft	Noise around airports		Congestion on access routes to airports
Marine & Inland Water		Modification of water system during port construction & canal cutting & dredging	Land taken for infrastructure; dereliction of obsolete port facilities & canals	Vessels & craft withdrawn from service		Bulk transport of fuels & hazardous substances	

Source: Organisation for Economic Cooperation and Development (1988b)

and Development (1988b), Button and Rothengatter (1992), and the case studies in Barde and Button (1990).

Any brief listing of the environmental implications associated with land-based transport is inevitably inadequate. Further, the effects of transport on the environment are complex (Linster, 1989). There are, for example, simple effects, both short and long term, which are caused by the responsible pollution before it undergoes chemical transformation in the atmosphere. Indirect effects occur on the natural environment after a mixture of pollutants have undergone an atmospheric transformation. Traditionally, attention has tended to focus on single forms of pollution but there is a growing awareness of these latter synergy effects and the damage done to the environment by cocktails of pollutants. The most serious problem is associated with photochemical oxidants that are formed by chain reactions between unsaturated hydrocarbons and other reactive organic compounds, nitrogen oxides and oxygen in the presence of sunlight. Ozone is the most prevalent photochemical oxidant. Cities such as Los Angeles in the US and Athens in Greece because of their geography are particularly prone to such problems.

3.3   The Main Forms of Environmental Impact
Accepting all the above caveats and difficulties, the following items, each accompanied by a few notes on their importance, are widely accepted as important transport-based sources of environmental degradation. A summary of some of the key, quantifiable points is also contained in Table 3.2.

Table 3.2
Summary of quantifiable environmental impacts of transport in industrialised countries

	North America	OECD Europe	Japan	OECD States
Air				
Total transport emissions as % of total emissions				
Nitrogen oxides (NO_x)	47%	51%	39%	48%
Carbon monoxide (CO)	71%	81%	na	75%
Sulphur oxides (SO_x)	4%	3%	9%	3%
Particulates	14%	8%	na	13%
Hydrocarbons (HC)	39%	45%	na	40%
Noise				
Population exposed to road traffic noise over 65dBA				
	19 million	53 million	36 million	110 million

3.3-1   *Noise.*

This is an especial nuisance in urban areas, in towns that suffer from a lot of through traffic (e.g. located astride major trunk arteries, such as rail lines, motorways, etc.) and at locations around transport terminals, such as airports, bus stations, car parks. Noise is, for example, often cited as the main nuisance in urban areas. The problem is not a new one and one of the earliest studies of the subject in the UK by the Wilson Committee (UK Office of the Ministry of Science, 1963) reported that the London Noise Survey conducted in 1961 had found that more people - 36 percent by road traffic, 9 percent by aircraft and 5 percent by railways - were adversely affected by noise than by any other source of nuisance. More recently, in the pre-unified FRG Frenking (1988) found 65 percent of the population were adversely affected by road traffic noise, with 25 percent seriously affected - by way of comparison this represented twice the problem of noise from neighbours and three times the problem from industrial noise. It should also be remembered that noise is not just generated by traffic but extremely high levels of noise are also often associated with the construction of transport infrastructure - up to levels of 110bB when piles are being driven (Independent Commission on Transport, 1975).

Measuring noise effects in a useful scientific manner poses problems because it is not simply the volume or pitch of noise that causes problems but also its frequency, duration and variability. The context in which the noise occurs is also important and, for example, the nuisance is likely to be greater in a residential area at night than in, say, an industrial estate during the working day. The Wilson Committee concluded that noise levels measured in A weighted decibels exceeded for 10 percent of the time (L_{10}) provided the best indicator of discomfort but this is far from an ideal measure.

It has been estimated (see Table 3.2) that about 110 million people in the industrial world are exposed to road traffic noise levels of more than 65 dB(A), a level considered unacceptable in OECD countries. While consistent data is somewhat sparse, there is also ample evidence that there are, in large part because of the nature of national land-use patterns but also because of differing national legal structures, quite considerable differences between countries in terms of the populations affected by transport-related noise - see Table 3.3. Equally it is difficult, because of data limitations, to discern exact trends in population exposure to high noise levels. International comparisons provide tentative evidence of a decline in numbers suffering from serious noise problems (i.e. over 65dB(A)) in some countries but arise in others, but there does seem to be a pattern of significantly increasing numbers of people falling into the 'grey area' of intermediate noise nuisance of between 55 and 65dB(65) (Organisation for Economic Cooperation and Development, 1991c). Equally, studies in the Netherlands suggest that the number of people claiming moderate disturbance

Table 3.3
Exposure of national populations to transport noise (percentage)

Country	Year	Outside noise level in Leq (dB(A))														
		Road transport					Aircraft					Railway				
		>55	>60	>65	>70	>75	>55	>60	>65	>70	>75	>55	>60	>65	>70	>75
Australia	...	46.0	...	8.0	...	...	...	...	...	...	...	...	...	...	...	...
Japan	1980	80.0	58.0	31.0	10.0	1.0	3.0	1.0	0.5	0.2	0.1	...	...	...	...	...
France	1985	54.4	33.1	6.6	5.5	0.6	...	...	...	...	...	...	...	...	...	...
Germany	1985	45.0	26.7	12.5	5.1	1.1	...	...	1.0	...	0.2	18.0	8.4	2.9	0.8	0.1
Netherlands	1987	54.0	20.0	4.1	1.3	...	36.0	15.0	0.4	0.1	...	6.0	1.5	0.6	0.3	0.1
Switzerland	1985	53.7	26.3	11.7	4.1	0.7	2.0	1.0	0.6	0.7	...	23.4	13.0	5.9	2.5	0.9

Source: Organisation for Economic Cooperation and Development (1991c)

from road traffic noise rose from 48 percent to 60 percent between 1977 and 1987.

Noise has several different effects on health and well-being (Organisation for Economic Cooperation and Development, 1988b). It affects activities such as communication (speaking, listening to radio and TV) and sleep. These effects further induce psychological and physiological disorders such as stress, tiredness and sleep disturbance. Noise can also contribute to cardio-vascular disease and, at high and prolonged exposure, hearing loss.

3.3-2 *Vibration.*

All large surface transport vehicles create vibrations as they move, especially where there are uneven travelling surfaces (Whiffen and Leonard, 1971), and aircraft do so at low altitudes during take-offs and landings, causing disturbances to the air. Road freight transport poses a particular problem in urban areas composed of fragile historic buildings. But in general, vibration can also have adverse effects on those living in houses close to transport infrastructure; in terms of disrupting their sleep which in turn can have health implications as well as affecting their general enjoyment of life.

3.3-3 *Accident risk.*

Transport is a dangerous activity. These accidents can concern not just those involved in transport itself but also third parties. The dangers inherent in the transport of dangerous and toxic substances are, in fact, increasing this latter problem (Organisation for Economic Cooperation and Development, 1988a). From a purely statistical perspective this is mainly seen in relation to road transport where there are, on a day-to-day basis, many fatal and serious accidents. Less frequent, but from a public perceptions perspective, more alarming because of the degree of potential severity associated with each incident, are rail, maritime and aviation disasters.

Some indication of the order of magnitude of the risks involved in transport is the fact that road accidents cost some 48,800 lives in the US and 7,967 lives in the FRG during 1987 and 10,961 in France during 1986 while in the UK 5,052 people were killed on the roads in 1988 with a further 63,000 seriously injured. In Italy, between 7,076 and 9,308 people were killed in 1986 (the number depending upon whether deaths are measured at times of accidents or a week later - see Ponti and Vittadini, 1990) and 213,159 injured.

It should be pointed out, however, that in many developed countries the number of fatal road accidents is decreasing - e.g. the figure for the UK is the lowest since 1954 and that cited for the FRG for 1987 should be compared with 19,139 in 1970. Data relating to the US is to be found in Table 3.4 and again shows that, despite many more road accidents (which rose from 16 million in 1970 to 18.8 million in 1984) the number of fatalities and injuries has declined. This is not, how

Table 3.4
Transport accidents and resulting deaths and injuries by type of transport in the USA, 1970-85

	Motor vehicles* (thousands)	Rail†	Commercial aviation	Waterborne§
Deaths				
1970	52.6	765	-	-
1975	44.5	575	221	243
1980	51.1	584	143	206
1981	49.3	556	132	154
1982	43.9	512	320	223
1983	42.6	498	89	289
1984	44.3	598	102	113
1985	43.8	454	638	69
Injuries				
1970	2,000	21,327	-	-
1975	1,800	54,306	109	97
1980	2,000	62,246	74	176
1981	1,900	53,003	82	141
1982	1,700	37,638	98	271
1983	1,600	32,196	49	209
1984	1,700	35,660	67	134
1985	1,700	31,617	73	57

* Data on deaths are from US National Highway Traffic Safety Administration and are based on 30-day definition.
† Deaths exclude fatalities in railroad-highway grade crossing accidents.
§ Covers accidents involving loss of life or injury causing a person's incapacity for more than three days
Source: US Department of Transportation

Table 3.5
Road accidents in India

Year	Total accidents (thousands)	Fatalities (thousands)	Injuries (thousands)	Fatalities per 10000 motor vehicles	Fatalities per 10000 population
1966	74.0	8.7	48.7	79.2	1.8
1971	120.0	15.0	70.7	80.4	2.7
1976	125.0	17.8	82.5	65.9	2.9
1981	161.0	28.4	114.0	54.9	4.1
1986	211.0	40.3	175.7	39.4	5.3

Source: Indian Ministry of Surface Transport, Transport Research Division (1986)

ever, the situation in many low-income countries where, as private transport is expanding, the number of fatalities continues to rise - Table 3.5 provides some details for road accidents in India. The increased amounts of hazardous waste transported in recent years, and the associated problem of spillage, is also adding to the risks borne by third parties throughout the world.

If one considers the accident rates by mode then road transport incidents dominate the statistics although, because of variations in modal split between countries, there are national variations in their relative importance. Some indication of the different accident rates by mode and over time for the US is, for example, given in Table 3.4. Interpretation of such data does, however, pose some problems. In particular, there is the point of comparison against which numbers of accidents should be set. Commercial aviation is, from a statistical perspective, generally cited as the safest mode of transport but this may not be the case viewed in terms of time exposure. Perrow (1984) makes the point clearly,

> Safety comparisons with other systems are hard to make. In many respects, commercial air travel appears to be much safer than automobile or rail travel. Many fewer people are killed in the first than in the other two. But an equally useful statistic would be the number of fatalities per hour of exposure, or per million miles travelled. Unfortunately, we do not have these statistics for automobile accidents ... if we used the statistic of fatalities per 100,000 hours of exposure, highway travel would be the safest mode of transportation .... One's chances of being killed while driving a car is only one per cent in fifty years of driving. We simply do a lot of driving and very little flying giving us the impression that the risk of the latter is much smaller.

3.3-4 *Atmospheric pollution.*

Transport is a source of many harmful gases (see Table 3.6 for a brief summary of some of the types of damage done). In relative terms transport is one of the major contributors of these atmospheric pollutants (e.g. see the details of the situation in the Netherlands set out in Table 3.7). Further, it is worth emphasising that while in some respects the environmental damage done by transport is increasing, in others there are reductions. In the Netherlands, for example, nitrogen oxides and particulates emissions have grown rapidly in recent years but there has been a modest decline in hydrocarbon emissions and, in absolute terms, in sulphur dioxides.

It is also worth remembering that exhaust fumes have a time and areal coverage (Himanen *et al*, 1992). There is a time gap as the impacts move from one level to another. Figure 3.1 offers a broad picture of what happens. At the higher levels, the original impacts are connected to many other effects and systems, which are not exclusively related to transport. A potent cocktail of transport- and non-transport-related emissions, therefore, often exists. For ease of exposition, however, we deal with each of the main pollutants separately. The discussions below provide some indication of both these long- and short-term implications, as well as the nature of the spatial coverage, when this is particularly relevant.

Table 3.6
Summary of environmental damage done by traffic

Pollutant	Source	People	Effects on Vegetation/ecosystem	Climate	Materials/buildings
Hydrocarbons	Incomplete combustion, carburetion	Direct, notably carcinogenic effects of individual components	Through build-up in, soil, feed and food crops	High greenhouse potential (methane) ozone formation	
Nitrogen oxide	Oxidation of N2 and N-compounds in fuel additives	Irritation, morphological changes in respiratory system	Acidification of soil & water, over fertilizing, increased risk of leaf & root damage	Very high greenhouse potential (NO_2), ozone formation	Weathering erosion
Ozone	Photo-chemical oxidisation with NOx and HC	Irritation of mucus and respiratory system, premature aging of lungs	Increased risk of leaf & root damage	Very high greenhouse potential	Decompostion of polymers
Carbon monoxide	Incomplete combustion	Inadequate oxygen supply, in particular heart/circulation and central nervous system		Indirect through ozone formation	
Particulates	Incomplete combustion, source specific emissions dust thrown up	Damage to respiratory system, toxic content with broad range of effects	Reduced assimilation		Dirty buildings
Soot	Incomplete combustion	Carcinogenic			Dirty buildings
Carbon dioxide	Combustion			Qualitatively important greenhouse gas	
Noise	Engine, drive and rolling noise	Substantial nuisance, higher health risk			Reduced value

Table 3.7
Percentage of some atmospheric pollutants attributable to transport in the Netherlands

Pollutants	CO	C_xH_y	NO_x	Particulates	SO_2
1970	74	6	34	7	2
1986	61	41	50	20	5

(i) *Fuel additive emissions.*
To enhance engine performance, additives are added to fuels. While some are relatively benign in their environmental effects others have caused increasing concern over time. Ethylene dibromide and ethylene dichloride (which are added to gasoline, together with lead, to increase volatility) have been found to be carcinogenic in animals and potentially so in humans. The organic lead compounds added to gasoline as an anti-knock agent, especially when used by automobiles in confined urban spaces, have been singled out for particular attention. Lead is a metallic element that can be retained in the body in the forms of its compounds and can have an adverse affect on the mental development of children and affect the kidney, liver and reproductive system.

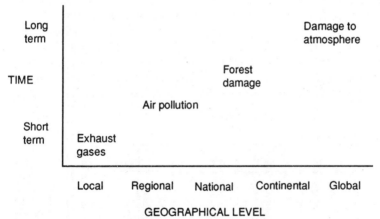

Figure 3.1
The time and areal coverage of exhaust gases

In industrialised nations, transport is the single largest source of lead emissions with some 50 percent of Pb associated with transport but the figure can approach 100 percent in confined urban spaces. However, the tightening of maximum lead content in gasoline laws (e.g. in the UK's case from 0.84 grams per litre to 0.40 per litre in 1981 and a further reduction to 0.15 grams per litre in 1985) and the fostering of increasing use of lead-free gasoline through fiscal measures has caused major changes in recent years.

(ii) *Particulate matters.*

These embrace fine solids or liquid particles found in the air or in emissions such as dust, smoke or smog. Sources include the fine asbestos and other particles stemming from wear and tear of tyres and brakes as well as matter resulting from engine, and especially diesel engine, combustion. Transport is the major source of particulate emissions in many industrialised countries including the UK.

Particulate matter may be toxic in itself or carry toxic (including carcinogenic) trace substances absorbed into its surfaces. It also imposes costs on physical structures, e.g. in terms of the need to clean and re-paint buildings

(iii) *Carbon dioxide emissions.*

The environmental concern here is in relation to carbon dioxide's possible climatic impact, for example, it is generally viewed by scientists as a major contributor to the greenhouse effect and consequential global warming (for a discussion of the economics of global warming see Schelling, 1992). CO_2 emissions result from the combustion of fossil fuels. The contribution of CO_2 to the atmosphere varies considerably between countries but the industrialised countries as a whole are responsible for about 80 percent of the total.

Much of the gas comes from the burning of tropical forests (about 15 percent), from chemical production (about 20 percent) and from the direct production and consumption of energy (about 40 percent). Estimates suggest, however, that about 15 percent of the world's total man-made emissions of CO_2 is generated by motor vehicles and in some OECD countries the figure may reach 40 percent. In the UK while transport is currently responsible for about 16 percent of emissions (some 31 million tonnes), it is the fastest growing source and 98 percent of this is associated with road transport - see Table 3.8.

Table 3.8
CO_2 emission sources in the UK

Source	1978	1983	1988	Change 78-88(%)
Domestic	23	23	24	4.4
Power stations	58	52	52	-10.3
Refineries	5	5	5	0.0
Other industry	50	38	37	-26.0
Transport	23	24	31	34.8
Other	12	10	9	-25.0
Total	171	152	158	-7.6

Since CO_2 is a natural constituent of air (although only about 0.03 percent) it is not strictly a pollutant. Additionally, excess amounts of the gas have no detrimental effect on personal health. The problem is that there is mounting, although some would argue not yet conclusive, evidence that high levels of the CO_2 in atmosphere, by preventing heat from escaping from the planet, will lead to global climate changes.

> In particular, the retention of heat by the earth and atmosphere owing to CO_2 in the air being 'transparent' to incoming short-wave radiation but 'opaque' to the longer wave radiation back from the earth. It is called the greenhouse effect because the glass in a greenhouse acts in a [similar] heat retentive way. (National Society for Clean Air, 1989).

The issue is not really one about the merits of the greenhouse effect *per se* (without it estimates suggest the global average temperature would fall to about -19°C), but rather about the desirability of the effects changes in its intensity will have. The exact geographical impacts of global warming and their timing are difficult to predict and the long-term economic consequences even harder to foretell (Nordhaus, 1991). After all, it is a global phenomena and little previous data exists to refine theoretical models. The types of problems which are feared, however, include:-

- a rise in the sea level as a result of thermal expansion of the sea and the melting of land ice;
- changes of climatic zones e.g. of desert regions and regions affected by tropical storms;
- global damage to forests due to climatic changes which worsen the existing impacts of NO_x emissions;
- detrimental effects on water resources in many areas;
- problems of adapting agricultural production;
- changes in tundra, boreal forests and permafrost areas which could lead to additional emissions of CO_2 and CH_4 and thus lead to further global warming.

(iv) *Nitrogen oxide emissions.*
These pose particular difficulties when combined with other air pollutants or in areas where residents already suffer from ill-health. In the latter case they can lead to respiratory difficulties and extended exposition can result in oedema or emphysema. At the transboundary level, NO_x emissions converted to nitric acid and combined with SO_2, form a significant component of 'acid rain' (or acid deposition) which has serious detrimental effects on ecosystems. The problems have been summarised by the Organisation for Economic Cooperation and Development (1988b), namely,

> Decreases in the pH values of fresh water bodies, indicating higher acidity, have occurred throughout Europe and North America. As a result, there has been a decline in or an elimination of the fish population in acidified lakes. Some evidence suggests that essential nutrients can be removed from sensitive soils releasing metals that are toxic to plants. Based on a growing body of research, it has been suggested that this mechanism may be responsible for very substantial damage to the West German forests.

About 50 percent of NO_x emissions stem from the transport sector, and the rest from the energy and industrial sectors although in many countries their output is falling. In the UK it is the fastest growing source of emissions, rising by about 2 percent per annum.

(v) *Carbon monoxide emissions.*

CO can have detrimental effects on health because it interferes with the absorption of oxygen by red blood cells. This may lead to increased morbidity and adversely affects fertility and there is evidence that it affects worker productivity. CO is especially a problem in urban areas where synergistic effects with other pollutants means it contributes to photochemical smog and surface ozone (O_3). Concentrations of O_3 at lower levels have implications for the respiratory system.

CO emissions result from incomplete combustion and some 90 percent of all CO emissions originate from the transport sector and about 80 percent is associated with automobile use. The figure reaches 100 percent in the centre of many built-up areas. Additionally, in countries such as the UK if the trends of the 1980s continue then emissions will grow by about 2 percent per annum in the future.

(vi) *Sulphur dioxide emissions.*

Emissions of this colourless but strong-smelling gas can result in bronchitis and other diseases of the respiratory system and they are the major contributor to 'acid rain'. Transport is directly responsible for about 5 percent of total SO_2 emissions with diesel fuel containing more SO_2 per litre than gasoline. What is more important, coal-fired electricity generation is a major source of this gas and thus there are further transport implications both for electric rail transport and the manufacture of transport vehicles.

(vi) *Volatile organic compounds.*

These comprise a wide variety of hydrocarbons and other substances (e.g. methane, ethylene oxide, formaldehyde, phenol, phosgene, benzene, carbon tetrachloride, chlorofluorocarbons and polychlorinated biphenyls). They generally result from incomplete combustion of fossil fuels, although evaporated gasoline from fuel tanks and the carburettor is increasingly contributing to releases of aromatic HCs such as benzene.

When combined with NO_x in sunlight, hydrocarbons and some VOCs can generate low-level ozone - the main component of photochemical smog. Besides producing respiratory problems and causing eye irritations, some of the compounds are suspected of being carcinogenic and possibly mutagens or teratogens (which can result in congenital malformations). For example, benzene emissions are both odorous and have been linked with certain forms of cancer such as leukaemia. About 80 percent of all benzene emissions originate from gasoline-powered vehicles. Further, chlorofluorocarbons, containing both chlorine and fluorine atoms, are seen as partly responsible for depletion in the ozone layer in the ozonosphere that leads to increases in ultraviolet radiation and, in turn, skin cancer. CFC emissions are from foam used in vehicle construction and from mobile air conditioning systems. VOCs may also have adverse effects on plant growth and result in deterioration of other compounds such as rubber.

Excluding methane, emissions of which largely stem from agricultural sources, about half of VOC emissions in industrialised countries are generally associated with road traffic and the proportion, with the exception of the US, tends to be rising (Organisation for Economic Cooperation and Development, 1991b). About 30 percent of all HC emissions are directly related to transport.

3.3-5 *Excess depletion of natural resources.*

While there is no economic reason not to exploit non-renewable resources at an appropriate rate, distortion in the market and political framework suggests that many such resources (e.g. hydrocarbon fuels, ecosystems, land, natural areas, etc.) are being over exploited. Excessive exploitation of carbon-based fuels is often seen as the major problem.

Table 3.9
Energy efficiency of transport modes

	Number of persons carried (% laden)	Energy (MJ) per passenger mile	Energy (MJ) per passenger mile (fully laden)
Petrol car			
<1.4 litre	1.5	2.79	1.05
1.4-2.0 litre	1.5	3.21	1.20
2.0 litre	1.5	4.96	0.87
Diesel car			
<1.4 litre	1.5	2.42	0.91
1.4-2.0 litre	1.5	2.96	1.11
2.0 litre	1.5	3.93	1.47
Rail			
InterCity	338(60%)	0.77	0.46
InterCity 225	289(60%)	1.04	0.62
InterCity 125	294(60%)	0.95	0.57
Super Sprinter	88(60%)	0.89	0.53
Electric suburban	180(60%)	0.70	0.42
Bus			
Double-decker	25(25%)	0.83	0.28
Single decker	16(33%)	1.40	0.47
Minibus	10(50%)	1.15	0.57
Express coach	30(65%)	0.61	0.40
Air			
Boeing 737	100(60%)	3.90	2.34
Motorcycle	1.2	3.13	1.80
Moped	1	1.31	1.31
Bicycle	1	0.10	0.10
Walk	1	0.25	0.25

Source: Hughes (1990)

In OECD countries road transport in 1987 directly accounted for 682 MTOE of oil consumption or 47 percent of the total - this represents a rise from 446 MTOE in 1970. This, however, takes no account of the full cradle-to-grave energy requirements of building and using an automobile or of providing and maintaining the associated infrastructure. There are significant differences in the energy efficiency of different transport modes and Table 3.9 provides some tentative estimate of the total energy use per mile by various modes of transport in the UK for 1988 (and Table 3.10 offers an indication of the costs per kilometre for some lower-income Latin American countries where transport technology is generally less advanced). Although these data include non-carbon-based energy inputs it is quite clear that overall use of carbon fuels is extremely high. The real question, which is not easily answered, is to what extent is this excessive?

Table 3.10
Transport costs per kilometre for selected South American countries

	Columbia	Brazil	Argentina
Automobile	3.17	3.24	3.99
Commuter rail	na	0.36	0.98
Bus	0.59	0.33	0.59
Taxi	na	na	5.69

Source: Inter-American Development Bank (1982)

Urban sprawl reduces land for nature conservation, recreational and agricultural uses and leads, because of increases in average trip length, to further high levels of travel demand with their associated environmental implications. Linked with this, transport infrastructure itself takes up considerable space - in the states of the pre-unified FRG 5 percent of land is given over to transport and in the Rhine-Ruhr agglomeration 10 percent of land is given over to transport infrastructure although in some agglomerations the figure may reach 60 percent (Blum and Rothengatter, 1990). Besides raising questions of exploitation of non-renewable land resources, this also has serious implications for such things as drainage and water ecology.

3.3-6 *Community severance.*
Communities are often divided by major infrastructure developments, especially in residential urban areas, which can result in social fragmentation. While some elements of the adverse effects this has on the local environment are encapsulated in such things as accident statistics and the state of the local atmosphere there are also often significant social implications for the quality of life which segmented communities can enjoy. Urban motorways or rail lines can make it difficult for members of the community to interact and participate fully. There are obvious problems of measurement and quantification

involved here but in the US, for example, Appleyard (1981) found a strong impact of residential street traffic on neighbourhood life and that urban expressways, especially when elevated, can be detrimental to the functioning of neighbourhoods, to wildlife and to enjoyment of open space.

3.3-7 Water pollution.
(i) Ground water.
Transport affects ground water systems in two main ways. First, transport infrastructure involves a substantial land-take. This affects drainage patterns and the water table with consequential implications for wildlife and, in the longer term, has knock-on effects on agricultural production. Second, surface transport generates particulates and other matter that directly pollute water courses but can also, through drainage actions, lead to soil acidification and other forms of soil pollution.
(ii) Maritime.
Transport impinges on the maritime environment not only through much publicised spills of oil and chemicals and the excessive discharge of waste, all of which harms wildlife and spoils beaches, but also through the coastal land-take required for the construction of ports and other facilities. In terms of water pollution directly associated with shipping, globally about a million tonnes of annual oil pollution stems from maritime sources (both from accidents and from tank cleaning). The level of pollution is, however, decreasing (see Table 3.11). While many spillages are small individually and result from a number of sources, most of the major spills resulting in significant local environmental damage are associated with marine accidents. The evidence is that the level of accidental marine spillage has stabilised in recent years, partly because of the reduction in the amount of oil carried as alternative, mainly pipeline, facilities have been developed and partly because of new legal requirements governing locations and methods of tank cleaning.

Table 3.11
Maritime oil pollution sources

Cause	1981	1990
Bilge and fuel oil	310,000	250,000
Tanker operational losses	710,000	160,000
Tanker accidents	410,000	110,000
Marine terminals	70,000	50,000
Total	1,500,000	570,000

Source: National Research Council (1991)

In terms of terminal facilities, ports require significant land-takes and, in addition, there is often a need for dredging that poses problems both for the immediate marine life and at dumping sites. The latter is becoming an increasing problem as bigger ships (e.g. the post-Panamax container vessels) mean that dredging requirements are more extensive and widespread than in the past.

3.3-8 *Congestion.*

While one tends to think of this as being primarily an urban transport issue, it is becoming an increasing problem at ports and airports where inefficient use is made of time, which has a positive value, and environmental damages in terms of atmospheric pollution, accidents, noise, excessive fuel use, etc. are compounded. Strictly, excessive traffic congestion, while an externality in the economic sense (see Chapter 5), really involves a lack of internal efficiency of the transport operations rather than being a form of environmental problem as conventionally understood. It is its close association and generally close correlation with pollution and other environmental concerns that makes it a topic of interest.

Quantifying levels of excess congestion is not easy given the difficulty of defining the optimal level to use as a bench-mark. (This is a problem we return to in Chapter 4.) The traffic speeds in some cities (e.g. Athens) are now as low as 7 to 8 kms per hour while in Paris they are only 18 kms per hour and 20 kms per hour in London.

3.3-9 *Visual intrusion and aesthetics.*

Problems here can stem from both transport infrastructure and the vehicles using it. While the two concepts are closely entwined, visual intrusion is strictly the blocking out of light or pleasant views by transport activities while aesthetics is rather more concerned with the actual design and style of the transport facilities. Both ideas embrace an entire life-cycle concept and, besides the actual working facilities themselves, embrace such things as the eyesores often associated with the disposal of old 'hardware', including disused infrastructure such as docks and railway lines and scrapped vehicles. To give some idea of the magnitude of this problem, in the latter context, in the Netherlands some 455,000 cars are scrapped each year yielding about 750,000 tonnnes of solid waste. Of this, 450,000 tonnes is recycled and the remainder, a nondecomposible mixture of metals, oily products, paint, plastics and other materials is dumped.

3.4   Evolving Trends

There is little doubt that transport imposes severe strains on the environment and, although there have been some successes in containing a number of problems, there are fears that the situation will, without some form of appropriate remedial action, worsen with time. There are a number of reasons for suspecting this and here we focus on only some of the key points that are being raised in debates.

3.4-1 *Economic integration in Western Europe.*

The economies of the established industrial world and those of newly industrialising countries (NICs) seem likely, subject to periodic fluctuations due to trade-cycle effects, to continue to expand into the future. This trend will, at least into the next century, be reinforced by the movement towards the Single Internal Market within the European Community and the more general opening to trade being facilitated by the creation of the larger European Economic Space. Also, in North America closer integration of economies brought about by trade agreements between the US and Canada and Mexico will foster economic expansion there. The natural growth in trade that is likely to accompany these developments will in itself create demands for more transport services with their associated environmental implications.

A lot has been written on probable impacts for transport of the creation of the Single European Market after 1992 and certainly the new situation has implications for transport and the environment not only within the Twelve and with regard to a number of transit countries, such as Austria, Yugoslavia and Switzerland but also to countries involved in the larger European Economic Space. But, how many of the changes taking place strictly have to do with the Single Market *per se* and how many with other, ongoing pressures to develop a true EC Common Transport Policy as explicitly set down in the Treaty of Rome, is difficult to decide.

In many ways the entire packages of measures currently in place or about to be introduced (Button, 1992b) are unlikely to offer any real solution to the underlying long term transport problems of Western Europe. While the measures to date have removed many of the former institutional constraints that limited the efficient supply of transport services, they have done little to ensure that the use and provision of transport infrastructure approach optimality in either an economic or environmental sense. In particular, while they are likely to produce some increase in the overall efficiency of the use made of transport infrastructure, and further EC-supported investments will provide some additional capacity, they will not be sufficient to meet the forecast growths in traffic.

The forecasts are that, with the continuation of existing policies, road traffic growth will continue and in the case of, for example, Great Britain may rise by up to 142 percent between 1988 and 2025 (UK Department of Transport, 1989c). Predictions made on a similar basis for the Netherlands suggest a 72 percent growth between 1986 and 2010. In the past, more aggregate studies of the EC have forecast significant growth in road haulage, especially international traffic, as manufactured goods take an ever-increasing share of the overall amount of goods transported (Gwilliam and Allport, 1982). The creation of the Single Internal Market will add to this if, as forecast, it leads to a 4.5-7 percent rise in the Community's GNP - an increase of 30-50 percent in transfrontier lorry traffic alone being predicted. A study for the European Parliament (Romera, 1991) forecast the overall growth in land transport will be 34 percent between 1988 and 2000. The European Conference of Ministers of Transport suggests an even higher rate amounting to 3.5 percent per annum into the next century.

Equally, if one looks at European aviation a similar picture emerges with traffic growing from 321.3 thousand million passenger-kilometres in 1978 to 507.9 thousand million by 1988 and forecast, by the International Civil Aviation Organisation, to rise to some 850 thousand million by the end of the century. We also already find that of the 46 largest airports in Western Europe, 12 are currently operating at or around their physical capacity and a further 11 will, it is predicted, reach capacity by 1995. Further, the EC and others have identified a series of major bottle-necks in the European surface transport networks and if traffic grows as forecast this number will expand and the problems intensify.

The underlying problem is that under current policies the efficiency of the transport system will inevitably deteriorate in Europe as congestion develops. The implications of this are summarised in a recent report submitted to the EC Commission (Group Transport 2000 Plus, 1991), *viz.*:

> ...a general deterioration in transport conditions due to inefficient use of the networks and the saturation of certain infrastructures (especially road and air). Also - albeit not so immediately noticeable - there is an on-going increase in the nuisance caused by transport. The culprit here is not so much network saturation as the actual increase in traffic.

Linked to this problem is the realisation that while there may be difficulties with congestion of existing facilities, and as we see below massive expansions in capacity are unlikely to be the answer although these are planned (e.g. see Table 3.12), there is a need to develop entirely new transport networks in Europe (Roundtable of European Industrialists, 1987). This stems both from the changes taking place within the EC, its probable expansion of membership and the almost inevitable links that will gradually be created with the post-communist states. There are forces, therefore, at work within the EC which indicate the concurrent needs both for restraint measures to make better use of the transport infrastructure available in the face of rising demands leading to excessive environmental degradation, and for the creation of new transport networks.

3.4-2 *Changes in Eastern Europe.*

The liberalisation of Eastern Europe, coupled with the new political geography that is emerging, represents both problems and opportunities for the environment of the countries in the region. It means in particular that the overall 'transport market' in Europe will expand considerably in line with major new urban and industrial centres being brought within the market system. It means, therefore, that many more major transport links must now be considered as part of Europe's transport future. In many ways this may prove advantageous for the long-term development of European transport since it creates something more akin to a natural market for transport services than currently exists. Environmentally the future is less certain.

Table 3.12
Intended infrastructure investment in the 1990s (million ECU p.a.)

	Netherlands	Germany	France
Highways	700	2,400	6,000
Rail	400	1,700	1,200
Waterways	200	400	300
Airports	200	100	300
Total	1,500	4,600	7,800

Short-term problems are likely to arise because of the attitude regarding transport that has grown up in Eastern and Central Europe over the past forty years and the impact this has had on the physical transport infrastructure now in place. In particular, the transport systems of Eastern Europe are dominated by rail (which itself suffers from low productivity and over-manning), tend to be of poorer quality than in Western Europe and have been developed since the late 1940s to meet the trading patterns of the members of the Council for Mutual Economic Assistance (Button, 1991b).

Regarding trade patterns, the bulk of foreign trade has been within the confines of the CMEA with much less taking place with the rest of the world. In 1985, for example, Bulgaria exported (in $US terms) about five times as much to other CMEA countries as to the rest of the world combined and imported four times as much. In the case of Czechoslovakia the ratio was about 3.5:1 for both exports and imports and about 1.5:1 for the USSR and 2:1 for the GDR on a similar basis. Additionally, the trade that existed between the former CMEA countries and the EC, in particular, while relatively balanced in financial terms was heavily biased in favour of bulk movements from Eastern Europe in physical terms. These trade patterns inevitably led to transport infrastructure being designed to cope with the particular form of internal CMEA trade. Forecasts suggest that on the basis of even a relatively conservative scenario, by the early part of the next century this pattern of trading activity will be transformed and with this will come the need for a different form of transport provision (Seidenfus, 1991).

In mode terms, the Eastern European states have been, especially in comparison with EC members, heavily reliant upon rail for freight transport (see again Chapter 2) but, in addition, their systems tend to be old and the efficiency of operations is highly questionable. While the Eastern European economies have extensive rail networks, a relatively small percentage of them are double-tracked. It is also clear that there is a need, in economic terms, for more electrification. For example, of 27,284 kilometres of line, 11,669 are currently electrified in the states of pre-1990 FRG but out of 14,024 kilometres in the old GDR only 3,475 kilometres were electrified and in Poland, of 26,545 kilometres only 6,296 are electrified.

In physical terms, the road systems in Eastern Europe are not much better. Not only is the amount of motorway-grade road very limited but the general quality of the system is poor. In this latter respect the United Nations Commission for Europe feels that,

> The present road infrastructure in Central/Eastern European countries has deteriorated such that it is unlikely to be able to cope with increased road traffic volumes (Lehmacher, 1990).

Equally, the vehicles using this network are less technically sophisticated and less environmentally friendly than those found in Western Europe.

There is already a momentum at work to increase investment in improved infrastructure in Eastern Europe. Germany is putting resources into the up-grading of the former GDR rail network, although the costs appear to be massive. One estimate, expressed in May 1990 by Dr Reiner Gohlke, president of the Bundesbahn, at a conference of the Community of European Railways, is that some DM100 billion is needed simply to get the old GDR rail system into a condition comparable to the network in the West. The European Bank for Reconstruction and Development (EBRD) sees the improvement of the transport infrastructure of the post-communist states as one of its main functions and indications are that it is going to commit a substantial part of its own resources to this end.

Table 3.13

Estimated NO_X emissions (10^3 tonnes per annum) for post-communist European states

Country	All modes 1980	Road transport 1980	Road transport Forecast 2000
Bulgaria	89	88	185
Czechoslovakia	91	88	95
GDR	-	81	144
Hungary	100	75	142
Poland	190	185	201
Romania	-	85	105

Source: Laikin *et al* (1987)

The outcome of these developments could, in both narrow economic and wider environmental terms, be a highly efficient transport system in the post-communist states. In the short term, however, the very rapid increase in car ownership and the switch from rail to road freight transport has the combined potential for increased atmospheric pollution and additional damage for the local environments, especially in urban areas, of these countries. Even predictions prior to the collapse of the communist governments in the region indicated major increases in transport-related atmospheric pollutants (Table 3.13).

3.4-3 *The developing world.*
Within the industrialised nations there have been major initiatives to seek policies to contain the adverse effects associated with transport. The absolute level of traffic of all kinds in these countries combined with projected growth rates makes the concern understandable. Often one also finds passing reference to the mounting problems in the lower-income countries but relatively little work has been undertaken to examine either the likely future scale of the environmental damage done by transport in these countries or of the possible policies for containing it. There are good reasons for thinking that this neglect may well prove inappropriate (Button, 1992c).

It would be naive to pretend that our current knowledge of the exact magnitude of environmental degradation associated with transport in low income countries, let alone our ideas of the future, is anything but very imperfect. Some fairly reliable guesses have, however, been attempted. Transport in developing countries, for example, has been estimated to account for about 4 percent of the global emissions of CO_2. Equally, estimates suggest that they contribute about 30 percent of the global emissions of harmful toxic pollutants - i.e. CO, NO_x and HC - and a somewhat greater proportion of lead and diesel particulates, the latter arising because of the generally lower quality of fuel used and the relatively larger number of diesel vehicles in the vehicle fleet. As mentioned earlier, transport is generally less safe in low-income countries. In general fatal accidents run at around 10 to 20 times the rate found in European countries and are now one of the major causes of death in many of these countries. Traffic accidents also impose considerable costs in the form of medical and other care - it has been estimated that this runs at between one and two percent of GNP in developing countries (Ross and Mwiraria, 1989).

The environmental problems associated with transport in low income countries are particularly acute in the rapidly expanding urban areas. It is here that some of the worst congestion and atmospheric pollution in the world is to be found. The pollution caused by motor traffic regularly exceeds the guide-lines set down by the World Health Organisation (WHO). The cities most seriously affected include Ibadan and Lagos in Africa; Mexico City, San Paulo and Santiago in Latin

America; Bangkok, Bombay, Jakarta, Manila, Seoul, Medan and Klang in Asia; Ankara, Cairo, Istanbul and Teheran in the Middle East and most of the cities in post-communist Eastern Europe.

It is perhaps useful to cite case study material to illustrate just how severe the transport-induced environmental problems of many low-income cities have become. In the Mexico City Metropolitan Area, for instance, there are now some 2.6 million cars and 0.6 million commercial vehicles and of this fleet it is estimated that about 43 percent of cars are over 10 years old. These vehicles are fuel inefficient and maintenance is poor. The quality of roads and track and the high levels of traffic congestion lead to stop-start driving with its adverse effects on fuel consumption. As a consequence, it is estimated that transportation is responsible for up to 61 percent of non-methane HC emissions, 64 percent of NO_x and 97 percent of CO emissions. In terms of energy consumption it is clear, if we refer back to Table 3.9, that if the car ownership levels in developing countries began approaching those in Western Europe or North America, energy consumption, and consequently pollution, would rise dramatically. In the three Latin American countries cited in that table, which are not the poorest by any means, one finds that automobiles account for only 25-35 percent of traffic at present but some 65-75 percent of the energy used in transport. While one can point to a wide dispersion in the mode split between developing countries, in contrast to the South American countries, for example, in Malaysia some 40 percent of households use a car for the trip to work while in Lae, Papua New Guinea, the figure is 15 percent (Sathaye and Meyers, 1987), the key point is that on average the car-use figure is still well below that found in industrialised countries.

The longer term perspective is not immediately encouraging. The situation is that as incomes rise then there will be a very significant rise in car ownership and use - indeed in many cases at rates well above those in most industrialised countries. Table 3.14 provides recent forecasts, based upon the use of quasi-logistic models, of future car ownership levels for some of the world's poorest countries under different assumptions regarding their economic growth. What seems to be emerging is that while the growth at the very lowest-income range is likely to be relatively modest, there is a high probability of a take-off in vehicle ownership and growth in those slightly richer nations where the prospects of economic development are much more positive. Linked with this, increased affluence will also inevitably mean more freight transport with the bulk of this going by diesel-powered trucks.

A significant feature of most low-income countries in recent years has been the secular drift of population into urban areas (see Table 3.15). This has been brought about partly by agrarian reforms but also reflects, often misguided, views about the prospects of employment and income. The result, however, has been a very significant growth

Table 3.14
Forecasts of car ownership in less developed countries (1986=100)

Country	Assumed Annual Rate of Per Capita Income Growth	Index of Car Park		
		1986	2000	2025
Burkina Faso	1%	100	143	286
	4%	100	183	394
Rwanda	1%	100	177	499
	4%	100	224	951
Togo	1%	100	149	335
	4%	100	205	751
Haiti	1%	100	96	161
	4%	100	128	351
Pakistan	1%	100	148	340
	4%	100	196	739
Cameroon	1%	100	162	440
	4%	100	255	1309
Gabon	1%	100	215	632
	4%	100	355	1922
Algeria	1%	100	141	341
	4%	100	232	1000
Mauritius	1%	100	146	209
	4%	100	219	544
Malaysia	1%	100	149	284
	4%	100	216	628

Source: Button and Ngoe (1991)

in car ownership and use in cities (Button and Ngoe, 1991). Indeed, historically, the growth of car ownership in the largest cities in Third World countries was already of the order of 7-15 percent in the decade 1960 to 1970. Added to this, the actual cost of transport in these cities has risen significantly with households spending 5-10 percent of their income on transport, and in some cases 15 percent, and city governments spending 15-25 percent of their annual budgets on transport investments and operations.

Looking forward, the situation in the urban areas of the developing world is inevitably going to get worse. The mid-1980s saw eight of the largest cities in the world with populations of over 10 million located in low-income countries. Predictions are that this number will have doubled by the end of the century while an 18 further agglomerations in the developing world will have populations of between 5 and 10 million. What this means is that without some major policy initiative, some 300-400 million urban dwellers in developing countries will be subjected to serious and dangerous air pollution within a decade.

A major difficulty is that the growth of urbanisation and the level of motor car ownership and use are closely linked (Faiz *et al*, 1990). This is to a large extent due to the concentration of wealth and money incomes in the urban areas of the developing World. It is also, though, influenced and entwined with the geographical spread which urbanisation generally entails and the resultant increase in the average

Table 3.15
Urban population growth in less developed countries

	1980	1985	1990
World	39.5	42.2	45.2
Developed Countries	70.3	71.6	72.6
Developing Countries	28.9	32.8	37.1
Africa	27.8	30.6	33.9
Asia	26.3	30.1	34.4
Latin America	65.0	68.5	71.5
North America	73.9	74.6	75.2
Europe	70.4	71.9	73.4
Oceania	71.2	70.7	70.6
USSR	63.0	65.2	65.8

Source: United Nations (1991)

length of trips which results. Comparing Nairobi and Mexico City, for example, shows average trip lengths of between 1.5 to 2.8 miles for the former while those for Mexico City, which is much larger, are between 3.5 and 6.0 miles. Public transport is much less efficient at serving a spatially dispersed market and hence the automobile, with its associated environmental problems, is used more often

Equally, the growth of commerce and trade within cities also brings forth additional commercial traffic and with it even higher levels of pollution associated with diesel engines. The general picture obtained from the extrapolation of ongoing trends is that by the turn of the century the pollution associated with motor vehicles in the major cities of developing countries will be well in excess of that currently found in urban areas of industrial countries.

4

Evaluating the
Environment

4.1   Introduction

Reducing the multifarious adverse environmental effects associated with transport to a common denominator is difficult. It is, however, important if one is to judge their relative significance. Various scales could be adopted but the putting of monetary values on these effects has the major advantage that it allows direct comparison with the costs and revenues which are normally perceived by those making decisions as to whether to use transport or not and, if so, which mode to favour.

One of the major criticisms of evaluation in the past has been that the techniques and procedures available were often unscientific or biased. Where economists had developed consistent sound theoretical approaches many were not convinced that they could be operationalised. In the past twenty years or so the picture has changed quite markedly and many governments now regularly deploy monetary valuations of external environmental costs in their decision making. Academics also now seem more confident that the techniques that they have developed offer useful practical tools in decision making - one just has to compare the rather pessimistic position expressed by Fisher and Peterson (1976) in their major review of the state of environmental economics in the mid-1970s with the recent up-date by Cropper and Oates (1992) to see how the world has changed.

It is still not, however, an easy process to put money values on the preservation of environmental amenities. At the most general level a number of stages must be gone through before it is even possible to approach an evaluation.

Figure 4.1 sets out a simple schema of how an evaluation may be attempted of the environmental damage done by emissions of NO_X from car engines. There is first the need for measurement of the emissions themselves. While this may pose only limited technical difficulties (although the history of monitoring carbon monoxide suggests these can be more severe than is sometimes thought) for individual vehicles, there are clear problems of aggregation over traffic streams and in conditions where there are adjacent (e.g. coal-fired power stations) sources of the pollution. With many gases these types of problem are compounded when synergy effects occur as they combine in the atmosphere. Even if the emissions from cars can be measured with some certainty, for evaluation purposes there is then a need to set them in context by established ambient conditions.

The third stage offers even bigger challenges as we saw in the previous chapter and is the one about which we, in general, know less. Deciding upon the exact impact exhaust gas emissions of NO_x have on trees and lakes and then in turn on wildlife and recreational facilities poses serious problems. This is an area where there is not always scientific agreement. Of course, these problems become even greater when we consider some other environmental effects of transport such as CO_2 emissions on global temperatures and then the effects of this on the wider ecosystem or on the implications for health of greater concentrations of volatile hydrocarbons in the atmosphere. In many cases, the work in these areas is still speculative.

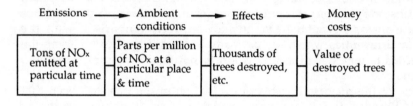

Figure 4.1
The chain of calculations to arrive at environmental evaluations

These stages, important as they are, fall outside of the sphere of economics, and within that of science and medicine, but it is important to recognise their existence before looking at the final stage in Figure 4.1, namely the final conversion of these physical costs into monetary values. A variety of ingenious and original ways have been devised by economists to do this and in some areas they have been remarkably successful in their work. One should perhaps make the point here that evaluation is only conceptually possible if the environmental resource is non-essential. Clearly, if the resource is essential then it has an infinite value. This, besides the uncertainty of the scientific evidence, is why much of the attention of those concerned with valuation has focused on relatively small changes in the environment.

Given the attention valuation of environmental effects is now receiving, some time is devoted to considering the economic concepts underlying current methodologies.

4.2   Total Value
Before looking at techniques for evaluating environmental attributes and the costs associated with environmental degradation it is

important to realise that, just like any other commodity or service, environmental services have a number of distinct features which confer benefits on society. These all, in turn, ideally require to have monetary values attached to them. A number of distinctions, therefore, need to be drawn prior to looking at techniques for evaluating them (Johansson, 1987).

First, there is the distinction between value in consumption and value in non-consumption. The former relates to the benefits associated with direct use of the environmental resource, e.g. the use of a valley for agriculture and fishing prior to a road being driven through it. Such use is generally, if usually somewhat imperfectly, captured in market values. In contrast, non-consumption use generally lies outside of the market, for instance, keeping with our example, the pleasure associated in bird watching or admiring the countryside in the valley prior to the road being built.

There may also be indirect non-consumption use. This can be through secondary sensations such as looking at pictures or films of the unspoilt valley even if it is never visited by the viewer or it may be because people simply gain satisfaction from knowing the unspoilt valley exists for others to enjoy. It has been recognised for some time that this latter existence value may be explained in a number of ways (Boyle and Bishop, 1985):

• *Bequest motive.* Following Krutilla (1967) it is often argued that people place a value on ensuring that environmental resources continue to exist for the utility of future generations.
• *Benevolence towards relatives and friends.* This represents utility gained by knowing that environmental resources are available to kith and kin at the present time.
• *Sympathy for people and animals.* People may have sympathies for other people who may suffer from environmental degradation caused by transport even if they have no personal link with these people.
• *Environmental linkages.* This relates to people's fears that any particular act of environmental degradation is simply a symptom of a wider malaise and that it is important to stop this degradation before this malaise worsens and does result in direct implications.
• *Environmental responsibility.* Some people take the view that they have a moral responsibility to protect the environment and should shoulder the costs of doing so.

The implication of this is that the calculation of the total value of any environmental resource requires the estimations of:-

total value = use values + indirect values + existence values

Environmental damage may affect the use values (including the indirect services) in a number of possible ways. Figure 4.2 offers illustrations. If a commodity is traded in a perfectly competitive market and an increase in environmental damage causes the value of that commodity to change (e.g. the need to install double-glazing to houses adjacent to a new road causes the cost of house construction to rise) then the loss of consumer's surplus is the shaded area to the left of the Hicksian demand curve shown in Figure 4.2(a). If on the other hand, environmental services are provided cheaply then congestion can arise or rationing is necessary (e.g. driving through the countryside) and the associated welfare loss is the shaded area in 4.2(b). If the environmental good is seen as a public good then a similar effect emerges and the loss to an individual of over-consumption is that seen in 4.2(c). The difference is that in 4.2(c) we are dealing with effects across many individuals, not just the single individual as in 4.2(b), and thus one must add the cost across all those concerned to obtain the true valuation.

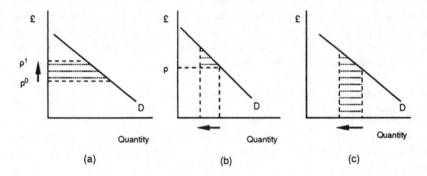

Figure 4.2
Measuring use value of the environment

4.3   Methods of Evaluation
A number of alternative approaches to valuation have been advocated and some quite widely adopted. At one level there are a number of *ad hoc* procedures which have no really common economic foundation but which have, in a number of studies and contexts, provided the basis for valuation of various environmental effects of transport, especially in the safety field. These are frequently based on such things as legal precedent, costs of 'insulation', lost production, etc. They are important, not so much from the intellectual perspective but rather from the fact that they have been used by groups lobbying for reform and by advocates in public forums such as road and airport inquiries. More recently rather more sophisticated and economically consistent approaches have begun to emerge.

Economic analysis has tended to involve two broad theoretical methodologies (Quinet, 1990). The first involves evaluating all community expenditures on transport including such things as the additional production costs caused by traffic noise. The difficulty here, as pointed out by Kanafani (1983), is that all impacts of transport must be included and then costs attributed. The second, and more widely used method, considers the marginal willingness to pay to avoid suffering the environmental degradation associated with transport. Inevitably care must be taken in applying these methodologies. In particular, they are mutually exclusive procedures and 'double-counting' problems may arise. Of course, while the methodologies have a relatively long pedigree in the economic literature, translating either into hard technique is another matter.

The actual applied science of evaluating environmental costs has developed considerably in recent years and now the application of revealed preference techniques, such as hedonic property price and wage risk analysis, and of stated preference techniques, such as contingent valuation, enables reasonable estimates of many environmental effects to be obtained. The aim here is not to offer a full discussion of the techniques available to place monetary values on these environmental effects - this is done very effectively elsewhere (Pearce and Markandya, 1989; Johansson, 1987) - but rather to give some indication of the main alternatives together with some discussion of their relative pros and cons.

4.3-1 *Precedents.*

Consistency over time is the prime reason for suggesting that historical precedents could be used as a means of valuating certain aspects of the environment. The normal understanding of historical precedents in this context are legal rulings on compensation for inflicting environmental damage. Compensation for deaths and injury in transport accidents is the most common application. The difficulties of such an approach, however, are such that it is seldom used in modern economic analysis.

First, the main applications have been in terms of valuing injury and death in transport accidents although there are instances of transport suppliers, and especially shipping companies, having to compensate for spillage of toxic pollutants. This is simply because precedents exist only where there are established rights and these extend to very few environmental attributes. Even if there was not this limit, the overall usefulness of the techniques is restricted by the nature of most legal systems. They normally apply to the need for victims (including relatives of people killed) of the incident to be cared for during the remainder of their lives. Consequently, where the environmental damage causes death the 'cost' to the deceased is not considered. Equally, damage to flora and fauna is generally outside of the scope of legal rulings on compensation. Third, where evidence has been produced looking at legal precedence it tends to show little by way of a consistent pattern.

4.3-2 *Averting Behaviour.*

Many adverse environmental consequences of transport can be ame-
liorated by various forms of insulation.   Noise nuisance, for example,
can be reduced by double-glazing of windows and accident risk by the
adoption of safer engineering design standards for transport infrastructure and the vehicles which use it. A widely deployed techniques for
assessing the costs of environmental damage is to equate them with
the cost of avoidance. Starkie and Johnson (1975), for example, attempted to seek a value for peace and quiet by assessing how much
people were prepared to pay to double-glaze their windows. Dickie
and Gerking (1991) have adopted the same basic idea from looking at
the costs of reducing air pollution by running an air conditioning unit.

The adoption of aversion behaviour generally involves a non-
marginal change in pollution levels. This is simply because air conditioning is fitted in a room or it is not. In Figure 4.3, the MC curves
show the marginal costs of healthy time (i.e. non-polluted days when
work is possible) with and without air conditioning - MC_1 being the
situation without air conditioning. Air conditioning improves air
quality and shifts the MC curve to the right. The normal method of
evaluation is to take area ABC as an indicator of the value of the environmental quality change. This represents the benefit from enjoying
the same amount of healthy time as previously after installing air
conditioning. It has the advantage that it can be calculated from the
cost function alone. The main limitation is the assumption that the
individual wishes to increase his use of healthy time (i.e. he may wish
to work more days).

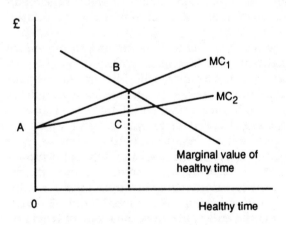

Figure 4.3
Benefits of a non-marginal reduction in air pollution

The practical limitations of such an approach are that it is difficult
to isolate specific expenditures on environmental grounds from the
implicit joint expenditure on other benefits accompanying, in our ex-

ample, double-glazing (e.g. reduced heating bills, etc.) or air conditioning (e.g. a cooler room temperature). The noise insulation, for example, is also only partial in that it does not offer protection when in the garden or when windows are open. More fundamentally, there are questions about the optimality of the level of avoidance adopted. In terms of safety, for example, the aviation industry provides an extremely safe product but only at a tremendous cost. In terms of potential lives saved each is implicitly valued more highly than, say a life saved on the roads where the per capita safety expenditure is much lower.

4.3-3 *Revealed preference: hedonic prices.*
While there are a limited number of instances where markets exist in environmental resources, there are circumstances where consumers of such resources, through their actions, implicitly reveal the values that they place on them. They make trade-offs involving sacrificing some monetary benefits to limit the use of environmental resources or gain some environmental benefit. In this sense they show a willingness to pay for certain environmental attributes. The classic case is the willingness of people to pay to live away from noisy airports or roads.

The underlying theory can be discussed in terms of Figure 4.4 which plots the welfare enjoyed by an individual at various levels of wealth. The diminishing marginal utility of money gives, for example, the trade-off curve I for an individual living in a quiet, rural setting. The construction of an airport adjacent to the house imposes measurable noise costs on this person and, for every level of wealth, this pulls the trade-off curve down i.e. it becomes II. If the person was initially at a point A on I then the imposition of the noise will reduce welfare to level B. To get him back to his original welfare level, compensation of BC would be needed, this being sufficient to move him around II until the original level of welfare is restored.

Some comments are needed on this approach. First, it does assume that there is a finite level of compensation which satisfies the individual. If, however, one starts at an initial position A^+ then it is not altogether clear this is so. (This type of problem essentially arose in the late 1960s when researchers were trying to value the noise costs of aviation at alternative sites for a third London airport - eventually an arbitrary value was adopted for some individuals). Second, the onus of the technique as described above is on compensation. One would normally get a different value by taking the amount required to be paid by the individual to bribe the authorities not to construct the airport (i.e. that necessary to get back to the higher trade-off curve I at the new level of welfare B). Strictly this approach is that of revealed preference since it is showing what sacrifice (or price) people will make for environmental benefits.

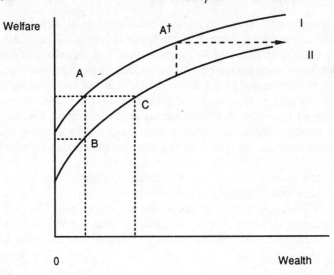

Figure 4.4
The wealth-welfare trade-off

In practical terms revealed preference techniques normally require fairly sophisticated econometric analysis. The problem is that most goods involve a variety of attributes of which the environmental elements only represent a sub-set. Indeed, most goods involve the use of several environmental resources. In consequence, the normal approach is to use an hedonic price index which puts values on the diverse attributes of the good being examined (e.g. the various features of houses in the noise case mentioned above). For example, if evaluating noise from an airport is the objective, then, using information on the characteristics of houses both close and distant from the airport, the following type of model could be used:

$$P = f(H, N, A, E)$$

where:- P is the price of each property; H is a vector of physical characteristics of each property (e.g. number of rooms, age, amenities, etc.); N is a vector of neighbourhood characteristics (e.g. socio-economic composition, residential density, etc.); A is a vector of accessibility characteristics (e.g. distance to town centre, proximity of schools, etc.) and E is a vector of environmental characteristics (e.g. noise levels, traffic accidents, etc.).

The exact specification of models differ, indeed one of the major problems with hedonic indices is that of model specification, but whatever form they take they seek to isolate the 'price' of each characteristic in the equation. This leads on to a second problem, namely it is necessary to have a substantial amount of information on the determinants of, in our example, housing selection processes just to gain an insight into the value of one environmental influence. It is also important that the characteristics used are the ones perceived to be important to house occupiers and buyers. It is not the actual set of characteristics which determine hedonic prices but rather the characteristics as seen by those active in the housing market. This is because we are using behaviour to evaluate attributes and behaviour is based upon perception.

Despite these, and some other limitations discussed below, the revealed preference technique has been widely used for a variety of evaluation purposes in transport. Noise we have discussed and some examples of values obtained are set out later. In addition, trade-offs between such options as fast, tolled roads and slower, untolled roads provide the basis for many valuations of travel time and, *ipso facto,* congestion costs. Again, decisions on safe, but more expensive travel options as opposed to cheaper but less safe options (e.g. regarding seat belt fitting) offer insights into the value of safety.

4.3-4 *Travel-cost method.*

New transport infrastructure can destroy recreation sites such as parks and fishing facilities which have been provided at a zero price. People, however, travel to such locations to make use of the natural amenities and thus incur a measurable travel cost both in terms of time and money. Use can be made of this information to gain some idea of the value of such facilities and, hence, the social cost of their destruction. In a sense this is a special case of the more general revealed preference approach but is often treated independently in the literature and this is the path pursued here.

Figure 4.5 offers guidance to the simplest travel-cost approach. Surveys find that the number of visits to, say, a park from an origin A amounts to X_a and from B to X_b. Further, the actual average generalised travel costs (i.e. including travel time costs) for these trips amount to P_a and P_b respectively from the two origins. A succession of further surveys looking at other origins enables the distance decay function to be derived. From this the consumer surplus derived from visiting the park and enjoyed by an individual living in A is seen to be area (A+B). Total surplus for those originating from A is then found by multiplying (A+B) by the number of trip-makers originating from there. Similar calculations can be carried out for each origin to get the aggregate surplus.

The method applied today is usually more refined than the simple one set out here (e.g. involving multiple sites and taking into account the characteristics of individuals) but the underlying concept remains. As with other techniques of evaluation, it is not without its limitations (Kealy and Bishop, 1986). Its main use is in evaluating specific types of environmental impact and is of less use in situations where there are a number of environmental factors involved and one wishes to evaluate them individually. It also tells us nothing about such things as existence value since only actual trips are considered in the

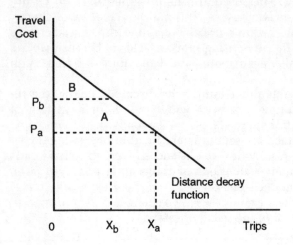

Figure 4.5
The basic travel-cost method

calculus. Perhaps a bigger problem, however, is the need to specify the generalised cost function which itself should include a monetary value of travel time. The work on the value of travel time is extensive but the subject is itself at least as controversial as that in the field of environmental evaluation.

4.3-5 *Stated preference.*
Direct market observation of the type used in revealed preference techniques has the clear advantage that one is dealing with observable trade-offs being made by individuals and society more generally. Revealed preference techniques also, however, have their limitations (Kroes and Sheldon, 1988):

• First, as indicated above, it is often difficult with revealed preference analysis to obtain information on the full range of choices open to individuals in terms of avoiding or mitigating the impact of adverse environmental effects.
• Second, and, in a way linked to the first point, revealed preference cannot easily handle new forms of environmental impacts or impacts of existing nuisances well outside the existing range.
• Third, it is assumed with revealed preference that those involved in choice situations have full information of what options are available or, at least, those conducting the research have a very clear idea of the degree of awareness which exists.
• Fourth, revealed preference techniques can handle qualitative information but tend to do so in a rather restrictive fashion.

Stated preference techniques (often called contingency valuations in the environmental literature) do not involve attempting to place values on environmental costs by observing trade-offs in the actual world but rather seek to elicit information on the trade-offs individuals would make when confronted with particular situations. They, therefore, have their origins in the area of market research and to-day interface with experimental economics where efforts are made actually to set up experiments to study human (and sometimes animal) responses to economic stimuli.

The most widespread approach is that of asking, through questionnaires, surveys, etc., a relevant group of individuals either what compensation they would need to keep them at their current level of welfare if some pre-defined transport-induced environmental degradation took place or, alternatively, what amount would they be willing to pay to prevent this occurrence (see Mitchell and Carson, 1989). The questions are set in an institutional context (e.g. to make it clear what methods of finance are involved) and, so as to provide a market framework, the questioner initiates the process by suggesting an opening 'bid' to which the respondent reacts.

The questions need to be couched carefully to ensure that the hypothetical trade-offs are clear and that the potential problems with the techniques (the main ones of which are listed in Table 4.1) are minimised. There are particular problems with individuals giving distorted answers (i.e. over- or understating true demand) when looking at public good values (e.g. the provision of quieter, more expensive road surfaces) in the hope that they will be able to 'free ride'.

Table 4.1
Sources of potential bias in the stated preference approach

Strategic	Incentive to 'free ride'
Design	• starting point bias
	• vehicle bias
	• informational bias
Hypothetical	Are bids in hypothetical markets different to actual market bids? Why should they be?
Operational	How are hypothetical markets consistent with markets in which actual choices are made?

Source: Pearce and Turner (1990)

At the strategic level, it is important that the opening bid is close to the final outcome since it tends to influence the reaction of respondents in the subsequent interactive process. Other types of difficulty involve the perception of the type of vehicle used for payment (or compensation). A pure value for some forms of transport-induced environmental intrusion should be independent of the method of payment or compensation used - it is the amount which is relevant. The problem is, thus, to select a neutral vehicle or at least to test the sensitivity of the evaluations gained to the methods of payment which could be used. Again at the strategic level the order in which information is presented to respondents coupled with its format can potentially bias results.

At a more fundamental level there are questions involving the extent to which the information gained through a stated preference approaches that which would emerge if an actual market did exist. Strict comparisons are not possible, since, by definition no actual market exists, but comparisons with other techniques can, at least, give some indication of consistency. In their analysis of a number of case studies (which were not transport specific) where stated preference techniques were deployed alongside other methods of evaluation, Pearce and Turner (1990) found that there was a 'reassuring' degree of overlap in the findings reported. Differences do, however, still exist and it is difficult to decide whether this reflects variations in the quality of individual studies or is a reflection of the usefulness of differing techniques.

4.4   The Environmental Costs of Transport
4.4-1. *Traffic noise.*
Perhaps the greatest environmental cost associated with transport in urban areas is the loss of comparative peace and quiet. It is possible to physically measure traffic-related noise nuisance in a generally accepted manner and, by application of hedonic price indices to the housing market, to place monetary values on it (e.g. Alexandre *et al*, 1980). Evidence from the US on traffic noise nuisance suggests values of between 0.08 percent and 0.88 percent of house price per one unit change in Leq, with somewhat higher values being found in Swiss and Canadian cities (see Table 4.2). In the context of non-land-based transport, similar values have been found for aircraft noise nuisance (see Pearce and Markandya, 1989).

A few attempts to put a global money value on noise damage, using hedonic prices, have been made: Pearce *et al* (1984) using a 0.4 percent depreciation index calculate a 1 to 2 billion French Francs (1980 prices) annual cost for traffic noise alone (i.e. 0.0035 to 0.007 percent of GDP) ; in Norway, Ringheim (1983) evaluates the loss of property values at 0.06 percent of GDP and Wicke (1986) estimates a total house depreciation of 1.9 percent of GDP for all noise sources i.e. about 1 percent attributable to transport noise only (according to Quinet, 1990).

4.4-2. *Atmospheric pollution.*
Estimating the costs of air pollution is particularly difficult, not least because the associated health effects are not yet fully understood (Horowitz, 1982). Also the long-term effects on the global ecology are only just beginning to be fully researched. Our exact knowledge of the damage done to agricultural crops as a result of atmospheric pollution is also not complete. Some information is, however, available and is

Table 4.2
The impact of noise on house prices (% of house price)

Location	Impact of one unit change in Leq
United States	
North Virginia	0.15
Tidewater	0.14
North Springfield	0.18 - 0.50
Towson	0.54
Washington	0.88
Kingsgate	0.48
North King County	0.30
Spokane	0.08
Chicago	0.65
Canada	
Toronto	1.05
Switzerland	
Basle	1.26

Note: Equivalent continuous sound level (Leq) equals a level of constant sound (in dB(A)s) which would have the same sound energy over a given period as the measured fluctuating sound under consideration.
Source: Pearce and Markandya (1989)

at least indicative. The overall impact of air pollution caused by transport has been estimated as accounting for between 17 percent in the US (Kanafani, 1983) and 30 percent in the pre-unified FRG (Schultz, 1987) of total air pollution. Translating such estimates into monetary costs yields a figure of $14 billion per annum (at 1989 prices) and between DM10 and DM17.5 billion per annum respectively. Retrospective assessments by Deakin (1990) suggest that these may be serious under-estimations.

4.4-3 *Congestion.*
This can generate excessive air pollution, waste scarce mineral fuels and is noisy. Its main cost, however, is in terms of the time wasted by those involved. Work estimating the money value of lost travel time has a long pedigree - information of such costs is of commercial value to public transport suppliers who may trade-off faster services against higher fares. The exact cost depends upon the mix of traffic and the reason trips are being made. Periodically crude estimates, of the type produced by the UK's Confederation of British Industry in 1988, are made of the total costs of time wasted in congestion (about £15 billion per year for commercial traffic) but these tend to suffer from major theoretical and measurement problems. In the CBI case the calculations were based on scaling up the responses to a small survey of distribution companies which were asked to assess the costs traffic congestion was imposing on their operations. Besides the small size of the sample and the inherent dangers of aggregation, there was no effort to

define a base-line level of optimal congestion as a basis for comparison nor was there any effort to net out the costs that the distributors were imposing on others but not paying for.

A more rigorous approach is to consider the opportunity cost of lost travel time. In the case of work time this is normally considered to be the lost production associated with being delayed in traffic congestion. In the case of non-work time revealed preference methods are widely adopted seeking to discover trade-offs travellers make between quicker but more expensive options and slower but cheaper ones. Using this type of methodology, in the UK the Department of Transport (1989a) has estimated values for an hour of time wasted in traffic congestion for a variety of different classes of traveller. The average value for all workers for working time losses is £8.416 (in 1988 prices) while for non-work travel time losses it is £2.075 per hour. Using the Department's figures, Newbery (1988) produced value of marginal congestion costs by road type in the UK (Table 4.3). These show the costs imposed by an additional vehicle joining the traffic stream. Aggregation gives an estimated annual congestion cost of about £12,750 million for 1989-90.

Table 4.3
Estimated congestion costs by road type in the UK

Road type	Marginal cost (pence per km)
Motorway	0.26
Urban central peak	36.97
Urban central off-peak	29.23
Non-central peak	15.86
Non-central off-peak	8.74
Small town peak	6.89
Small town off-peak	4.20
Other urban	0.08
Rural dual carriageway	0.07
Other trunk and principal	0.19
Other rural	0.05

Source: Newbery (1990)

Recent work in the USA has attempted, using traffic modelling techniques, to put a monetary value (in terms of travel time and excess fuel costs) on congestion for 39 urban areas (Hanks and Lomax, 1990). This produced values in the range from $5,240 million per annum for Los Angeles to $290 million for Minneapolis-St Paul. The city with the highest congestion cost per registered vehicle was Washington at £920 per annum.

4.4-4 *Accident risk.*

Accident risks are partly internalised within transport in the sense that individuals can insure themselves. However, many travellers have no insurance or, where it has been taken up, it is on the basis of a misperception of the risks involved. There are also third party risks involved in the possibility of accidents during the transporting of dangerous goods or toxic waste. Attempts to devise methods for valuing accident risk have a long history, especially with regard to fatal accidents.

The methods of valuation currently in use, however, still differ between countries. Some adopt cost avoidance calculations, others use lost production/consumption-type techniques but the use of revealed and stated preference methods is becoming more widespread. The lost production (or *ex post*) method essentially asks what output the economy foregoes if, for example, someone is killed in a road accident - essentially a discounted calculation of the difference between what that person could have been expected to produce over the rest of his life and what he could have been expected to consume. The obvious problem is that a pensioner's death would be accorded a positive value with such a procedure! The lost consumption (or *ex ante*) method avoids this problem by assuming that the individual would gain utility by not dying and thus does not net out lost consumption, the ability to enjoy this consumption acting as proxy for the welfare of remaining alive.

There is still not universally accepted value for accident prevention. For example, values of £0.5 million, DM1,240 million and $2-$7 million per life preserved by safer transport are now being used for policy making in the UK, the states of the pre-unified FRG and the USA respectively. Academic studies also show some variability in their results. A review of studies in the US, UK and Sweden using mainly stated preference methods (Jones-Lee, 1990) concludes that the most reliable estimates from such studies give a distribution of values of life in 1989 with a median of $1.1 million and a mean of $3.4 million. Even within countries the figures are not undisputed, however, and, for example, other evidence indicates that in the UK case a figure of over $750,000 per life would be a better estimate on a 'willingness-to-pay' basis (Jones-Lee *et al*, 1985).

Of course, not all accidents are fatal and, in many cases, only motor vehicles are damaged. In the pre-unified FRG, values are placed on reduced incidence of serious accidents (DM56,000 each) and on material damage (DM25,000 per accident).

While reservations must be expressed over the method of valuing lost life (in terms of lost production), and some of the other forms of accident damage, Table 4.4 provides an indication of the relative costs by types of accident in the US for 1980 and Table 4.5 provides the breakdown of values used in Sweden in 1989. These types of figures can also be aggregated to give national costs of accidents - e.g. this has been estimated as being 33 billion francs for France in 1986.

Table 4. 4
Societal costs of motor vehicle accidents in the USA ($ billion in 1980 prices)

Category	Fatal accidents	Accidents with AIS 1-5 injuries	Accidents with property damage only	Motorists uninvolved in accidents*	Total
Medical	0.07	3.26	-	-	3.33
Productivity	12.10	2.14	-	-	14.24
Property	0.17	3.83	16.98	-	20.98
Other	1.38	6.16	4.73	6.38	18.65
Total	13.72	15.39	21.71	6.38	57.20

* Insurance costs
Source: US National Highway Traffic Safety Administration (1983)

Table 4.5
Social costs of road traffic accidents in Sweden (Swedish krona, 1985 prices)

	Material costs	Humane value	Total costs
Killed	500	3,700	4,200
Severely injured	200	400	600
Slightly injured	25	15	40

4.4-5 *Aggregate approaches.*
While there has been considerable work on the valuation of environmental costs of transport at the case study level less detailed analysis has been conducted of the more general relationship between environmental costs and other, more traditional economic costs. One exception is the study of Quinet (1990) which attempts, in very broad terms, to assess the relative importance of the environmental costs of transport *vis-à-vis* the gross national products of the industrialised economies. He takes a broad view of environmental costs in the sense that his analysis includes: external costs (noise and pollution), partly internalised costs (safety) and costs borne by users (time and monetary expenses).

While there are both theoretical problems in defining the social costs of transport and in their subsequent monetary evaluation, Quinet (1990) has suggested a method of relating some of the key concepts. In Figure 4.6, the following are depicted in the top component of the diagram:- D(N), shows the total cost of noise nuisance to an individual at each level of noise emission and consequently it also represents the willingness of an individual to pay to reduce pollution from each nuisance level. (Hence, if the current level of noise is N_o then the individual is suffering II nuisance and would be willing to pay that amount to remove the noise. As drawn, it is assumed that the marginal willingness to pay for abatement falls as the nuisance level decreases and that there is a current level of noise N_m); A(N) represents the expenditure required to reduce a particular noise nuisance level of N_m to a nuisance level of N - it is assumed that the marginal abatement cost is constant and, again, that there is a current level of noise N_m; and T(N) is the summation of D(N) and A(N).

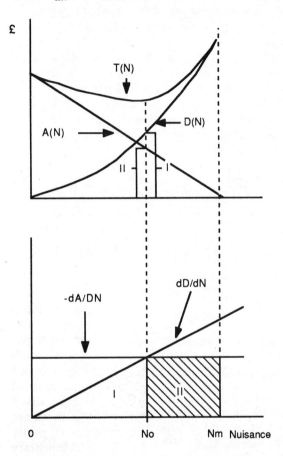

Figure 4. 6
The social costs of transport

The lower part of the diagram shows (strictly the negative of) the marginal abatement cost (dA/dN) and the marginal willingness to pay for abatement (dD/dN).

Assuming the initial level of nuisance is N_m then the optimal abatement which should be aimed for is that which minimises the combined cost of abatement and the willingness to pay for abatement, i.e. N_o in Figure 4.6. At this level of nuisance, those affected are willing to pay I to reduce the problem to N_o and the cost of doing so is II.

We see, from the lower diagram, that this is consistent with standard welfare economic theory that marginal cost (dA/dN) should be equated with marginal benefits (dD/dN) at an optimal situation. Since this lower diagram shows marginal curves we can define I and II as appropriate areas under them. The narrow definition of environmental costs generally relates solely to the abatement costs (i.e. an estimation of II) but a more comprehensive approach is to evaluate the costs of abatement to the optimal level coupled with the willingness to pay for removal of the remaining nuisance (i.e. I plus II).

Despite this effort to treat the environment in a logical and comprehensive fashion, Quinet admits his results, presented in Table 4.6 are only partial. In particular, there is no allowance for such items as visual intrusion, vibration, acid rain, etc. and longer-term effects, associated with such things as the greenhouse effects, are missing. The time costs are also, as he admits, gross figures rather than a reflection of time wasted due to excessive congestion.

Table 4.6
Broad estimates of the costs of selected environmental damage due to land transport (% of GDP)

Environmental problem	Costs	
	Road	Other modes
Noise	0.10%	0.01%
Pollution	0.40%	-
Accidents	2.00%	-
Time	6.80%	1.70%
User expenditure (including		-
infrastructure management)	9.00%	3.00%
Total	18.30%	4.71%

Source: Quinet (1990)

An alternative way of looking at the environmental costs is to consider how much transport costs would change if the costs of noise, pollution and accidents were internalised. Deakin (1990), has estimated that internalisation of air pollution costs in the US would increase automobile costs by between 6 percent and 12 percent per mile, of noise costs would add a further 0.5 percent to 1 percent and of accident costs (not already internalised) another 12 percent to 19 percent. This would add something like 20 percent to 33 percent to vehicle operating costs. The accuracy of the figures, as with Quinet's, must be treated with some caution. Further, Deakin does not attempt to embrace congestion costs, which are likely to be considerable, nor values of visual intrusion, vibration, community severance, etc.

5   Economic Causes of Environmental Degradation

5.1   Introduction

In this chapter we explore some of the conventional economic theories which have been advanced to explain why transport is responsible for excessive environmental degradation. It is very much concerned with why markets, despite their apparent success in more narrow economic terms in generating high gross domestic products, have proved deficient in many cases when it has come to ensuring sufficient protection for the environment.

The chapter differs from the one following in that we are not concerned with failures in government policy, other than that they do not create complete markets, but rather with the problems which can arise as a result of failures in the market itself. This is very much the traditional approach to environmental problems and it is the type of thinking which has tended to dominate transport policy in this field. How important strict market failures are *vis-à-vis* the problems created for the environment by government interventions in transport markets is difficult to say. Certainly, the mounting evidence from the post-communist states suggests that, as a generalisation, in those societies at least interventions in market processes have proved extremely damaging for the environment. The comparative dearth of research into intervention failures in western industrial economies makes any other than such broad statements on the scale of the two types of failure impossible. Further, the failures are themselves in reality often closely entwined with each other and separation is frequently impossible save in a very theoretical context.

The nature of the underlying problem with markets which interests us here has been neatly summarised by Theesuwes (1991),

> For a neo-classical economist environmental pollution is a prime example of market failure. The perfect competitive free market economy, in which individual consumers maximise their individual utility or welfare levels and private firms maximise their private profits given market prices for all goods and services will, under ideal conditions, reach a Pareto optimal social welfare position. This social welfare property of the free market economy is the exact analytical analogue of Adam Smith's intuitive notion about the blessing of the invisible hand in an economy where agents are only concerned

about private welfare. Environmental pollution, however, requires concern about the welfare of others and hence prevents the attainment of an optimal social position in a free market. In this sense the free market fails.

The intention here is certainly not to go into all of the theoretical issues surrounding externalities and related matters. The literature on this subject is enormous and there are many comprehensive texts on welfare economics which bring it together. Rather the aim is to provide some background material which sketches an outline of some of the central results found in this literature and to highlight, where useful, their particular relevance to transport.

5.2   The Traditional Framework

Since pollution is one of the main environmental disbenefits of transport it is useful to begin by setting out the standard economic model of where it fits into normal production theory (see, Cropper and Oates, 1992). In the jargon of environmental economics, it is seen as a public 'bad' which results from 'waste discharges' associated with the production of private goods. (Put simply, lead pollution in the atmosphere comes about as a by-product of the internal combustion of petrol which is being used as an input into a process aimed at moving about an individual.) Such a relationship can be expressed as:

$$U = U(X,Q)$$
$$X = X(L,E,Q)$$
$$Q = Q(E)$$

where; U is a vector of individuals' utility, X is a vector of goods consumed, Q is a vector of the level of pollution, E is a vector of the level of waste emissions and L is a vector of conventional factor inputs (e.g. labour and capital). Welfare is seen as dependent upon both the goods consumed and the level of pollution. As we can see, in this formulation, waste emissions are treated as simply another factor of production - in other words it implies that cutting back on such emissions will require additional inputs of other factors for abatement purposes. Put another way, reductions in E reduce output. Pollution also enters the production, as well as the welfare, function because of the direct detrimental effects it can have - this leads us on to a more detailed discussion of externalities in section 5.3. The level of pollution (Q) is itself treated as some function of the vector of emissions.

A standard refinement is to include the reaction of victims who expend resources to 'defend' themselves (e.g. wear smog masks in our lead pollution example) when confronted by pollution. The utility function may then take the form:

$$U = U[X,F(L,Q)]$$

where some factor inputs (L) are diverted from production for this defensive purpose. The level of exposure (F) is then determined by both the extent of the pollution and the amount of inputs used for protection.

One can use this type of framework to suggest optimal conditions for such things as levels of pollution and defensive expenditures by individuals. The former requires maximisation of the utility function subject to the production function and pollution constraints. The outcome is:

$$\frac{\partial X}{\partial E} = \sum \frac{\left\{\frac{\partial U}{\partial Q}\frac{\partial Q}{\partial E}\right\}}{\left\{\frac{\partial U}{\partial X}\right\}} + \sum \left\{\frac{\partial X}{\partial Q}\frac{\partial Q}{\partial E}\right\}$$

This shows that the creator of the pollution should extend its waste discharges to the point at which the marginal product of these emissions equals the sum of the marginal damages that are imposed on consumers (the first expression on the right-hand side of the equation) and on producers (the second expression).

In terms of defensive actions, the relevant condition setting out optimal outlays is:

$$\frac{\partial U}{\partial F}\frac{\partial F}{\partial L} = \frac{\partial U}{\partial X}\frac{\partial X}{\partial L}$$

which says that the marginal value of each input should be equated in its productive and defensive activities.

The environmental problem arises in this traditional framework because there is no price attached to environmental resources. In consequence, a producer will continue to pollute until the marginal return from doing so reaches zero (i.e. $\partial X/\partial E = 0$). In most cases this is beyond the socially optimal level. The problem can, therefore, be seen in terms of externalities - the costs which are not taken into account by the polluters.

5.3   Externalities

Theories concerning externalities have a long pedigree in economics. The definition of what constitutes an externality is rather slippery, indeed Baumol and Oates (1988) call it 'extraordinarily elusive'. At one extreme, for example, anything which results in a market not functioning efficiently, which would embrace monopoly influences, has been seen as an externality. This, though, is really too broad to be helpful. Perhaps the most cited definition of an externality, however, and the one which is of most use, is that advanced by Meade (1973):

> An external economy (diseconomy) is an event which confers an appreciable benefit (inflicts an appreciable damage) on some person or persons who were not fully consenting parties in reaching the decision or decisions which led directly or indirectly to the event in question.

From this, externalities, therefore, can be seen to have two important characteristics. First, there is interdependency involved - there is interaction between the decisions of economic agents. Second, there is no compensation paid so that the one who creates costs is not obliged to pay for it (nor in the case of a benefit, completely rewarded for it). This second point, however, is now sometimes thought inappropriate since it implies that the optimal policy is to remove or compensate for the externality altogether rather than to optimise its magnitude. One should also make the important additional point not incorporated in Meade's definition, namely that these spillovers must be unintended or an incidental by-product of some otherwise legitimate economic activity. They cannot, for example, be the results of a criminal action.

More formally, externalities can be said to exist when the utility function of an individual (or the cost or production function of a firm) depends not only upon the variables under his/her control but also on variables under the control of someone else where this dependence is not encapsulated in market transactions. Hence, for person J who is consuming private goods, $x_1^J, x_2^J .... x_N^J$ but whose welfare is also affected by activity x_1^K associated with person K, his utility function takes the form:-

$$U^J = U^J (x_1^J, x_2^J, ... x_N^J, x_1^K)$$

The external cost (or benefit) is measured as the difference between this and the utility function without x_1^K entering it.

These externalities can take a variety of forms dependent upon the combinations of producers and consumers affected. Road traffic congestion, for instance, is a consumer-upon-consumer externality since one motorist's trip is affecting the utility being enjoyed by another. In contrast, the noise created by a commercial aircraft taking-off is a producer-on-consumer externality. While much has been made of these distinctions, as Rothenberg (1970) has pointed out they are somewhat artificial. He takes the view that really one is dealing with generic congestion in the sense that they all have a common characteristic in as much as they involve people consuming in common form a public good where the presence of other users adversely affects the quality which that public good renders to each. In terms of environmental degradation, the implications are that there are too many people consuming a scarce resource to the detriment of all in the same way that traffic congestion stems from too many people using a given piece of road to the detriment of all.

In the standard static partial equilibrium short-run model, there are three broad ways in which externalities are treated in the economic literature - all yield the same result but place different emphasis on the underlying nature of the problem. Also, the different approaches tend to be used interchangeably in subsequent discussions quite simply because some points are easier to illustrate using one formulation rather than another. The differences in approach are illustrated in Figure 5.1.

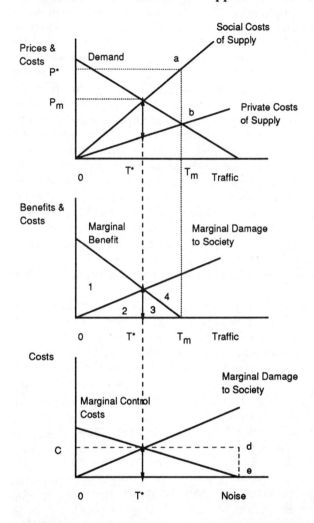

Figure 5.1
Alternative ways of looking at optimising environmental damage

The most frequently-used approach relates to basic supply and demand conditions for, in our case, the use of a road. In the top element of Figure 5.1 we have the private costs of supply curve and the social costs of supply curve where the former does not include externality costs of noise. The way the curves are drawn implies that pollution is cumulative, that none exists when there is no traffic and can be represented in a linear way - assumptions which are often quite reasonable although not inviolate. The area between the curves at any traffic flow is the total cost of pollution. The private market equilibrium in this case is a flow of T_m and a total noise pollution level of 0ab. If potential users of the road took into account their fall social costs then the flow would fall to T*. The implications of this, and a fact policy makers face, is that even at optimal traffic flows pollution does not fall to zero and that the actual social equilibrium imposes costs on road users in the form of a higher financial cost of road travel i.e. a rise from P_m to P*.

The intermediate element of Figure 5.1 looks at the private marginal benefit curve for road use associated with making different numbers of trips in a given time period. Assuming a competitive situation, this is developed from the top element of the figure as the vertical distance between the demand curve and the private costs of supply curve, i.e. P - MC. (It is often called the marginal net private benefit curve, a term we use frequently below). The marginal damage to society curve is the difference between the private costs of supply and the social costs of supply curves since it shows the level of noise pollution associated with level of traffic flow. Matching benefits and societal damage at the margin gives the same socially optimal traffic flow as in the top element, namely T*. To the left of this level extra benefits associated with the freedom to use noisy vehicles are outweighed by the social costs involved.

What a change from the free market outcome of P_m to P* illustrates in this case is that the introduction of measures to control of noise will not produce a strict Pareto improvement. Society benefits by suffering less damage from noise to an amount equal to the combined areas (3 + 4) but there are costs equal to area 3 which are borne by the road users. The fact that the former exceeds the latter, and hence compensation could be paid to road users adversely affected (if felt politically appropriate for distribution reasons) does, however, mean that the oft-used Hicks-Kaldor hypothetical welfare compensation criteria is met.

Finally, the problem can be looked at in terms of actual noise levels. In the lower element of Figure 5.1 noise is measured on the horizontal and associated costs on the vertical. The assumption is that reductions in the noise nuisance can only be made at an increasing marginal cost while, as above, the marginal damage to society curve is upward sloping. The socially optimal output of noise is where these two functions intersect.

While the technical approaches to externalities are useful analytical tools, and the different methods of presenting the same problem are often helpful in thinking through the implications of various policy approaches for handling them, they offer little beyond that. There are, however, a number of important distinctions which should be drawn between various forms of externality and the differences which can exist in various market structures. Nijkamp (1977) offers a useful and comprehensive taxonomy but here we content ourselves with a brief review of the distinctions which seem pertinent for the transport sector.

A first important distinction which must be drawn is that between what are generally called technological externalities and pecuniary externalities. The former are of the type outlined above where there are real resource costs (or with positive externalities, benefits) involved. These are the ones which tend to receive the greatest attention in the literature on the environment and are usually the rationale underlying particular policy actions. Pecuniary externalities occur when one individual's activity level affects the financial circumstances of another, but which need not produce a misallocation of resources in a world of pure competition. They are, therefore, essentially distributional and reflect interdependencies in economic systems. They do not affect aggregate economic efficiency but rather they affect who benefits and loses as a result of a particular market situation. As we see in Chapter 9 it may, in fact, from a policy formulation perspective be rather naive to ignore this type of externality as economists are often prone to do. We tend to follow tradition when looking at other distinctions and focus on technological externalities.

A second important distinction is between situations when the externality is separable and non-separable. An example illustrates the difference. If a new airport creates noise which forces office buildings to insulate themselves by installing double-glazing this results in a change in the fixed costs of production at such sites but, being a once-and-for-all cost and independent of the level of activity at the airport, it does not influence the marginal costs of production. In other words it is separable. Profits, however, and, in the long term, location and investment decisions, are obviously affected. Non-separable externalities occur when the marginal costs of one agent are directly affected by the actions of others. Traffic congestion would seem to fall into this category where the number, timing and routing of trips made by an individual is influenced by the congestion costs imposed by others. Technically, in these circumstances the externality not only shifts the individual's cost curve but it also changes its slope, i.e. the marginal cost changes. This poses particular problems for defining optimal remedial measures which imply the need to equate the ultimate marginal cost with price.

Third, Buchanan and Stubblebine (1962) distinguish between relevant and irrelevant externalities. An environmental externality is seen to be potentially relevant when the spill-over creates a desire on the part of the afflicted party to engage in trade, collective actions or some other means to change the situation. Essentially it argues that transport policy makers should only become concerned about environmental issues when potential relevance is established rather than be pro-active in seeking out what they think to be problems. The notion of relevance can be extended to include Pareto-relevant effects. These embrace externalities where the system can be adjusted in such a way that the adversely affected party can be made better off without the offending party being made worse off. Again, this may be of more importance to the political economy of the acceptance of environmental policy and distributional issues than the technical debate about such things as the economic efficiency of various policy instruments.

Finally, there is the distinction between private and public good externalities which until recently was held as important with respect to the exact nature of policies which should be pursued. The former is concerned with cases where the externality affects specific groups (e.g. the vibration and noise of heavy vehicles going down an unpaved country lane) while the latter involves externalities which affect everyone's welfare position (e.g. the health damage associated with lead in petrol). Put another way, private externalities involve depletable resources (i.e. one person suffering the noise of a passing vehicle means others some distance away do not) while the public externality is about undepletable resources (i.e. one person's inhalation of leaded air does not prevent others from inhaling it). The distinction was felt important because it meant that while private externalities may be most reasonably treated through combined taxes and compensation with public externality only taxation is practicable. As Freeman (1984) has rigorously demonstrated this distinction is not correct, and in both cases an appropriate Pigouvian tax (see Chapter 8) equal to the marginal social damage levied on the generator of the externality with no supplementary incentives for victims is a correct policy response.

5.4   The Question of Property Rights
Understanding exactly what causes externalities is important in appreciating the types of policy which may prove most useful in limiting any adverse effects associated with them. Perhaps the most important theoretical contribution in this area has come from the Nobel Laureate, Ronald Coase (1960), who highlighted the importance of property rights. These relate to the right to make use of a resource and these rights may be private, in the sense of belonging to an individual, or communal, in the sense that they are shared. The key problem which results in adverse environmental externalities is, in this framework, caused by the lack or the inadequacy of property right allocations.

Figure 5.2 provides a diagram depicting curves reflecting, at different traffic levels, the marginal net private benefit (MNPB) of road space to transport users and marginal external cost (MEC) stemming from local traffic-induced pollution imposed on those residents adjacent to the road. They are assumed to take the standard shape. The lack of any allocation of property rights to the environment will encourage transport users to make maximum use of it, i.e. traffic will be at level Q^t.

If, however, property rights to the environment were suddenly explicitly allocated to those subject to pollution (e.g. a 'right to peace and quiet' established) then the amount of traffic would in the very short term fall to zero. Quite simply, motorists would have no rights to cause pollution and hence could not use the roads. This, though, is not a stable equilibrium because at the margin when there is no traffic, the MNPB of road use by potential motorists exceeds the MEC of pollution to local residents. The incentive in a market framework, therefore, is for the latter to 'sell' some of the property rights to potential road users. (Another way to look at it is that road users would be willing to compensate those suffering from the negative effects of the externality at least the full cost of their discomfort in order to use the road.) Trade in property rights will, in fact, occur until MNPB is equated with MEC with a resultant traffic flow of Q*.

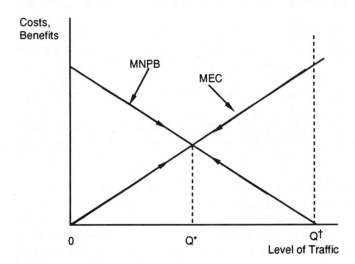

Figure 5.2
The importance of property rights

The outcome is exactly the same if the initial allocation of property rights goes to the road users. The immediate situation would be that traffic would flow at level $Q^\dagger$ but that in this case, because the MEC curve lies above the traffic MNPB at this flow, it is the afflicted who would be willing to pay the motorists to reduce their activities. Indeed, they would continue to be willing to pay them until the traffic flow is reduced to Q* after which the demands for additional monies on the part of the motorists would exceed the benefits to the residents of reducing the externality further and an equilibrium would be reached.

With the Coase model, from a pure efficiency perspective, it does not matter who has the initial allocation of pertinent property rights; the outcome of bargaining and trading is that an optimal level of pollution will emerge. (Of course, from a distribution point of view the outcomes are somewhat different in that the group allocated the property rights enjoys a windfall gain from the ability to sell them.) From a policy point of view, therefore, externalities can be removed without direct government involvement if property rights to environmental resources are allocated and trade in these rights is allowed.

While of considerable importance for examining the causes of externalities and pointing to potential solutions, the Coase theorem is not without practical difficulties.

• First, there are many forms of environmental degradation to which it is simply very difficult to assign property rights and for those with property rights to exercise these rights. Essentially the problem is one of excludability; it may prove very difficult to exclude those without appropriate property rights from making use of the environmental asset.

• Second, it does assume that there is perfect competition in the market for road space which is necessary for the conventional definition of MNPB (i.e. P - MC) to hold. If for some reason this does not hold then the necessary conditions for the bargaining solution to be optimal do not exist. While competition for road space may be considered relatively competitive and the problem a trivial one in this context, markets for landing slots at airports, use of rail lines, access to bus terminals, etc. are somewhat different and quasi-monopoly powers of various kinds are common.

• Third, in many cases the actual costs of trading, in terms of acquisition of necessary information, the conducting of the bargaining, etc. are so high that trade would simply not occur. The problem is essentially one of high transactions costs. In fact, however, since these costs involve genuine resource implications, it is quite possible to argue that it is optimal for the externality to remain if the costs of trade exceed the costs of those associated with the environmental damage. Equally, though, in many such cases, because of the nature of transactions costs, it may be efficient for the government to become involved more directly and to optimise environmental externalities through other policies.

6.1   Introduction

In recent years there has been something of a questioning about the underlying causes of environmental degradation. In particular, there has been increased interest in the ways in which governments intervene and manipulate markets. This questioning extends well beyond the transport sector and is much broader than just being concerned with environmental issues.   Nevertheless, transport does seem to be the subject of a considerable number of what have become known as intervention failures.

Government intervention failures may be defined as internal (e.g. concerned with allocative and X-efficiency) and external market failures (e.g. externalities *per se*) which result from inappropriate actions (whether deliberate or not) of government. They may usefully be divided into two categories. First, those which stem from the inadequacies of government (which need not be at the national level but may also be due to actions by either local or state authorities or, in a more global context, by an international agency) in correcting market failures. Second, those which embrace inappropriate policies elsewhere in the economy that actually worsen the environmental situation.   In particular, the latter often involve the pursuit of policies that are aimed at achieving objectives with no, or at least very little, direct environmental content but which do in fact have a negative environmental impact.

While useful in categorising problems, it should be recognised that in practice the distinction between market and intervention failures is a complex one. Since, for example, it is possible for government (or, in the international context, governments) to regulate markets, at the extreme, the level of the environmental problem could be said to be a policy matter. Government is ultimately responsible for allocating property rights and it is this allocation that determines the rate of exploitation of resources, including the environment.

Even where there are, so-called free, resources (such as the atmosphere and oceans) the decision to allow them to remain free is one of international policy and, indeed, on occasions some of these resources are brought within systems of control (as for example happened with the allocation of areas of air space with the arrival of aviation).

Viewed in this way, all adverse environmental effects stem from actions (or lack of actions) on the part of governments. This approach of treating all environmental problems as intervention failure is unifying in that it avoids the difficult problem of needing to draw strict 'boundaries' between market and intervention failures - economic ideas of market failure simply become one of several different possible forms of intervention failure.

Nevertheless, the distinction between the two broad forms of failure, market and government intervention, remains helpful when drawing up a framework within which to analyse the causes of environmental deterioration and in clarifying key causal linkages. The theoretical distinction is explored in more detail below.

6.2   The Concept of Intervention Failures
As we have seen, economic theory advances a variety of reasons for market failure with particular emphasis placed upon problems of inappropriate assignments of property rights (e.g. Knight, 1924 and Coase, 1960). In effect, the atmosphere, oceans, etc. are seen as quasi-public goods from which it is difficult to exclude potential users (that is. they may be considered free resources). Users of these 'free resources' are, therefore, not cognisant of the full marginal opportunity costs of their activities. Coupled with this, many markets where production involves substantial environmental damage would seem prone to excess capacity and, thus, over-supply because of inherent, internal imperfections (e.g. because they are intrinsically monopolisticaly competitive or because they operate under conditions of decreasing cost). With no governmental effort to ameliorate them, market failures would persist with their associated sub-optimality.

Government's failure to intervene, however, is much broader than that associated with straightforward failure to correct for market imperfections. Governments pursue a variety of objectives and, for a number of reasons (including the inherent myopic nature of many political systems), environmental protection may consciously be sacrificed in the pursuit of other economic goals (such as, protecting employment in specified industries, improving the balance of payments, stimulating a region's growth, etc.).

More frequently, however, the problem is that little account is taken of the potentially adverse effects on the environment of furthering these other goals and the negative environmental impact is essentially an accident, or a residual, of these other policies. Of course, in some instances, there may be positive side-effects on the environment of policies designed to have a direct incidence elsewhere although optimisation of environmental trade-offs would then only be coincidental.

The nature of the problem is made clearer by referring to Figure 6.1 which offers a schema showing the branches of regulatory activities which most governments engage in. We interpret regulation here to infer government interventions of all kinds. We focus on the micro-economic aspects of regulation, although in practice the intensity and forms of microeconomic involvement are often governed to a consid-erable degree at any point in time by macroeconomic policy. If the government, for example, is concerned with inflation, and believes that excessive public expenditures are contributing to this, then it is likely to look differently upon increasing public ownership or using subsidies as a market regulatory instrument than if there were defla-tionary pressures at work.

At the microeconomic level there are often trade-offs to be made at what one might consider the meso-policy level. This involves trade-offs between antitrust regulation, social regulation and, what we have termed, economic regulation. For example, increased emphasis on so-cial regulation may conflict with efforts to change the nature of compe-tition policy. Further down the tree, within the area of social regula-tion, environmental policies may result in trade-offs with consumer protection measures and even, in some instances, with health and safety-at-work measures. Moving down to an even lower level of ag-gregation, and one not depicted in the diagram, within environmental protection there may be conflicts in policy measures between transport and other sectors of the economy and even within transport itself. The key point is that trade-offs involving environmental matters, in-cluding those focusing on transport activities and industries, are often not made or are treated inadequately in the political process.

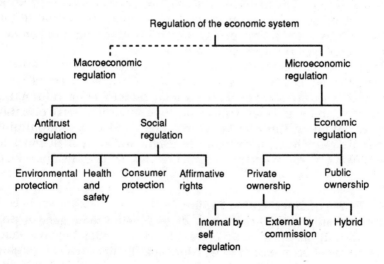

Figure 6.1
The branches of government regulation

This form of intervention failure should be distinguished from situations where government policies aimed specifically at ameliorating environmental damage may themselves be ineffectual or even prove harmful. The most serious of these cases is where the policy instrument employed is, because of inadequate knowledge, simply counter-productive. More common is the situation where in attempting to reduce a specific environmental problem, the policy employed generates a worse problem elsewhere or creates a different form of environmental damage. These are matters of inadequate information and uncertainty rather than strictly intervention failures. We return to discuss some of the main informational problems in transport policy making at the end of this chapter.

Packages of measures (e.g. containing pollution charges, emissions standards, pricing controls, etc.) have the further potentials for unpredicted interactions that may prove counter-productive. In many cases, such as the conflicting and technically impossible US goals of the 1970s to reduce automobile emissions by 95 percent and to achieve 27.5 miles per (US) gallon for automobiles, policy decisions of this general nature stem from crisis decision making and can be contrasted with more successful policies which enjoyed a longer gestation period - US automobile safety policy being a useful comparison (Crandall *et al*, 1986).

Equally, as we saw in Chapter 2, there are numerous levels of government (from international bodies such as the United Nations down to small local community councils) and also divisions of responsibility within governments (see Beckenham, 1985) and these levels and divisions can create conflicts in policy formulation. Even if environmental protection is an agreed objective it is quite possible for problems to arise if there is inadequate co-ordination of policies across the various bodies. Obviously, these problems are compounded if the different bodies pursue conflicting policies with some giving environmental matters a low priority and others a higher one.

In summary, the deterioration of environmental resources can usefully be treated as a function not only of traditional market failure but also as due to intervention failures (and sometimes to informational failures whereby policies with a positive environmental orientation misfire). While distinction between market and intervention failures is in some cases hazy, it seems to be useful and we will spend a little time looking at the relevance of intervention failures in the transport field.

6.3   Forms of Intervention Failure

In the text, an attempt has been made to develop some general principles to permit the drawing up of lines for demarcation between the different forms of economic failure. More specific lines may be drawn by looking at some key examples. Below, drawing upon fairly well-explored cases, the effects of several possible forms of intervention failures in transport are examined. In each instance, a specific government policy tool is considered to be adopted in the transport sphere for some non-environmental purpose and its potentially negative effect on the environment is illustrated.

6.3-1 *Incomplete charging of the full private costs of transport.*

A useful and pragmatic way of approaching the distinction between market and intervention failure is to consider the following simple example set out in Figure 6.2. Here actions by the consumer are deter-mined by the generalised costs (including any non-financial costs borne by the consumer) of the commodity purchased. In the standard literature on negative externalities (which goes back to Pigou,1920) the marginal social costs of production (MSC), which embrace negative environmental effects, are viewed as being more than the marginal private costs of production (MPC). The outcome is that, because the producer does not have to bear the external costs of his actions and thus reacts to the MPC rather than MSC curve, production is sub-op-timally high (i.e. at the point where demand equals marginal private cost, resulting in an excessive production of F - F° in the diagram). In consequence, a social welfare loss (assuming a constant marginal util-ity of money) equal to the area abc occurs due to the excessive environmental damage inflicted.

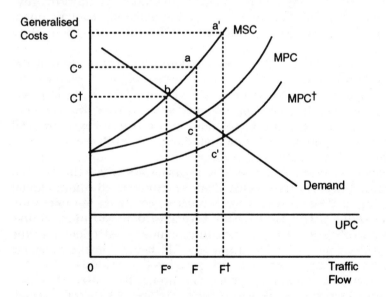

Figure 6.2
The effects of lack of adequate perception of private costs

If the Polluter Pays Principle (Organisation for Economic Cooperation and Development, 1975 and Alexandre *et al*, 1980) is adopted, then a charge of the amount indicated in the diagram would be levied on each unit consumed to internalise the pollution costs. The magnitude of such a charge in the transport context depends very much on individual circumstances but it seems unlikely that it would be inconsequential.

A crucial assumption of this type of analysis, however, is that the producer is fully informed about his own private costs of production. Equally, it is assumed that he bears the full private (i.e. non-environmental) costs of his activities. Intervention failure is generally typified by policies that violate one or other of these assumptions. For example, in the context of pollution generated by motor traffic, if the government provides the road track but charges for it in a manner which does not make the road user aware of his full private costs at the time the decision to make a trip is made (e.g. road users pay for their track costs through annual fees rather than direct tolls) then this will lead to traffic levels in excess of F in Figure 6.2. Equally, government subsidies to compensate transport users for some of their otherwise private costs will lead to a similar magnification of the traffic flow.

The general problem can be seen in the figure. The road user, because of some element of government policy, is unaware of or not responsible for some part of his private cost of trip-making. In this instance, and assuming for simplicity a constant marginal deviation of perceived from actual private cost, UPC represents the degree of 'misperception'. The result is that the reaction marginal private cost curve shifts vertically down to MPC^+ (i.e. MPC - UPC) and the traffic flow rises to F^+.

In terms of evaluating the relative magnitudes of market and intervention failures, this may either be assessed in traffic engineering terms as, respectively, the traffic flows $(F - F^o)$ and $(F^+ - F)$, or in economic terms (i.e. measured as lost economic surpluses) as the areas abc and a'acc'. It is not difficult to see that the welfare losses associated with a relatively small distortion stemming from intervention failures of this kind, can prove to be substantial.

It is useful to consider some of the circumstances where this type of intervention failure arises. One instance concerns the method of charging for road use. As we have already seen from the data presented earlier on methods of raising revenue from road users (Table 2.7) considerable sums are collected from annual licence fees. While strict hypothecation is seldom used (the US being something of an exception to this) many countries still perceive these charges as proxy road-user fees. The periodic payment of a licence fee, however, is unlikely to influence the use made of a road network. Further, the actual charges levied do not reflect the track costs of individual groups of road users - see details of the UK situation set out in Table 6.1. Thus, even if users were sensitive to the 'charges' imposed on them, they would not lead to an optimal traffic mix.

Another example was the system of tax relief afforded commuters in Germany (see Blum and Rothengatter, 1990). Table 6.2 sets out details of the tax allowances which people enjoy with respect to the costs of travelling to work. The justification for the concessions being compatibility with the self-employed whose travel expenses are tax deductible. The system changed in the late 1980s and, in fact, the tax effects are somewhat more complicated than the table indicates (Kunert, 1988). In particular, the impact of tax relief on travel to work must be treated in conjunction with 'lump sum tax allowances' and 'employment allowances' which merge into a 'general employee's allowance' in 1990. It also interacts with fuel taxation levels that have also changed as part of the overall fiscal reforms initiated in the late 1980s.

Table 6.1
Ratio of vehicle taxation to allocated infrastructure costs in the UK (1989)

Vehicle class	Tax to cost ratios
Cars/light vans/taxis	3.4:1
Motorcycles	2.3:1
Buses and coaches	1.1:1
Goods vehicles over 1.525	
Tonnes unladen:-	
Not over 3.5 tonnes GVW	3.1:1
Over 3.5 tonnes GVW	1.3:1
Other vehicles	2.4:1
All vehicles	2.6:1

Source: UK Department of Transport (1989b)

Table 6.2
Tax relief per kilometre for journeys to work (DM)

Mode	Allowances		
	1970-88	1989	1990-
Walk	0.00	0.00	0.00
Bicycle	0.00	0.00	0.00
Public transport	actual	actual	actual
Motorcycle	0.16	0.19	0.22
Car	0.36	0.43	0.50

Source: Blum and Rothengatter (1990)

The effect of the tax relief on journey-to-work costs, taking account of the full implications of the overall tax structure in Germany, is to distort the pattern of land-use activity one would anticipate with a consequential spreading of the population. In terms of specific environmental implications, Blum and Rothengatter have calculated the physical impact of the regime on different categories of transport accidents and on various forms of atmospheric pollution. The results are summarised in Table 6.3. In simple terms, the tax relief regime would seem to lead to additional accidents of all types on the roads and increases in emissions of the main forms of automobile pollutants. Translating these physical effects into monetary terms, Blum and Rothengatter (1990) estimate that the associated accident costs amount to some DM0.9 billion per annum and atmospheric pollution to some DM0.4 to 1.1 billion. Overall, it is estimated that the annual social cost of the measure is some DM1.5 to 2.1 billion.

Table 6.3
Estimated impact of Germany's journey-to-work tax relief regime

	Direct effects*	Indirect effects[†]	Total
Accidents			
Material damage (events)	6,671	3,185	9,856
Killed (persons)	317	0	317
Injured (persons)			
severely	2,462	689	3,151
slighty	5,204	3,703	8,907
Atmospheric pollution			
CO (tonnes)			164,910
NO_x(tonnes)			28,230
SO_2 (tonnes)			750
CH (tonnes)			27,960
Particulates (tonnes)			810

*   Due to impact of tax on level of travel
†   Resulting from changes in driving behaviour
Source: derived from Blum and Rothengatter (1990)

A further example of where government policy means private motoring costs are often poorly reflected in driver perception functions involves the tax relief given to company cars in countries such as the UK. The situation has changed somewhat recently but previous experiences highlight the nature of the problem

It was estimated in 1979 that the favourable tax arrangements in the UK meant that up to 70 percent of new cars sold are to some extent 'company supported'. (British Institute of Management Foundation, 1979). More recent estimates by the tax authorities, which take into account reforms to the tax regime which remove some of the advantages enjoyed by company vehicles users, suggest that some 10 percent of the total car stock in the UK consists purely of 'company cars' - this amounts to about two million vehicles in 1989 - although other official sources indicate the figure could be as high as three million. (For details of the tax relief offered see, Ashworth and Dilnot, 1987.) While it has been estimated that a fully-financed company 1.6-litre saloon car, used for 12,000 miles of private motoring a year, is worth a salary equivalent to £3,300 (and £16,300 if it is a 3.6-litre Jaguar) it is actually the company which benefits most from the tax regime. A firm could, for example, provide an employee with a 1.6-litre car in 1987 which would cost it, in discounted cash terms, some £1,670 per annum less (mainly because National Insurance premiums are avoided - estimates put the aggregate savings of premiums to companies to be in the order of £1 billion per annum) than paying the employee a comparable salary increase. The effect on car use is reflected in the fact that in 1981 some 37.8 percent of peak-period trips into London were by company cars being used for personal travel with a further 30 percent of commuters having either their mileage or maintenance costs subsidised by an employer. (Only 21.6 percent of automobile commuters were receiving no form of subsidy offering either themselves or their employer tax relief.) Additionally, the engine size of company cars, and hence their fuel consumption is on average (at 1.62 litres in 1989) larger than that of private cars (1.39 litres) indicating a higher per mileage fuel consumption.

6.3-2 *Policies affecting complements and substitutes.*
A similar type of problem to the above arises if a government subsidises or, with some other policy measure, reduces the price of complementary goods to transport (such as parking) or provides direct consumer subsidies (rather than fare subsidies to public transport suppliers). It may also arise if government keeps the price of competitive goods to transport (e.g. land at locations where residents would not need to undertake much travel) artificially high.

In these circumstances the demand for transport is shifted out *vis-à-vis* the free market situation. The outcome is seen in Figure 6.3 where Demand$^+$ can be thought of as the demand for car use with the cost of parking kept below the optimal level. Again there is an excessive traffic flow beyond the optimal level F which can be divided between that resulting from market failure (F - F$^\circ$) and that attributable to government policy (F$^+$ - F). The welfare measure of the social cost of intervention failure in this case is a'acc'.

6.3-3 *Public ownership and free access.*
In some instances policies to contain the potential distortions of market exploitation and offer a social service by means of public ownership and free access may generate external costs in excess of the private market outcome (DeMeza and Gould, 1987; Evans, 1992 offer a critical review of the particular graphical representation used by these authors). An example can help illustrate the point.

In Figure 6.4, the cost curves relate to the generalised (i.e. money plus travel time) costs of automobile trip-making on an urban road that has an engineering capacity flow of F*. We assume that the environmental impact of this traffic is closely correlated with the prevailing level of congestion. Following the conventional analysis of urban traffic flow (e.g. Walters, 1961), the Average Social Cost (ASC) of trip-

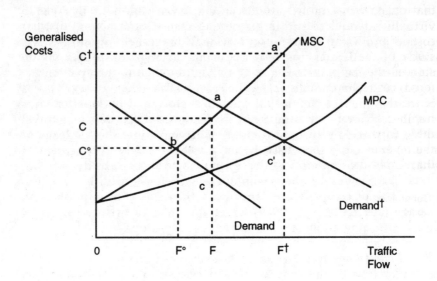

Figure 6.3
Demand distortions due to intervention failures in the market for a complement

making curve is drawn backward bending. This is a reflection of the effect of congestion build-up on the traffic flow. The flow F', for instance, may be associated with a low ASC of trip-making when the number of vehicles on the road is small and traffic is moving rapidly or with a high ASC when there is a large volume of traffic moving slowly.

Public ownership of the road with no form of entry constraint (e.g. through road pricing) will lead to a traffic flow of F' and an ASC of C'. Optimal road use would imply a traffic flow increase to $F^\dagger$ (i.e. a reduction in the traffic volume with the resultant increase in speed enhancing the flow to the point where the Marginal Social Cost (MSC) is equated with demand).

In this instance the public ownership of the facility and free access is clearly sub-optimal but it is an even worse outcome than that provided by a private monopoly supplier. A monopolist would set a toll for the road which would limit use to C" - the flow where MR = MSC and which would maximise monopoly rent. This would, however, be an overall generalised cost below that applicable in the free access situation and the traffic flow resulting would involve less congestion.

6.3-4 Excess capacity due to fare controls.
In many instances the motivation behind government intervention is to prevent exploitation of market power by the supplier of transport services and, at the same time, ensure market stability. Fares and the number of suppliers in the market are, therefore, regulated to ensure

that only normal profits are earned by those licensed to operate. In virtually all cases of such regulation the fares set are based upon the costs of providing the transport service. However, as Panzar (1983) in a study of the US civil aviation industry has shown, in these circumstances the supplier is left with a large number of possible trips offered/cost combinations all of which would yield only normal profits. Since the costs of trips being offered by the supplier rise with their number beyond some efficiency level and, because the demand for these trips will decline as the regulated fare rises in unison with costs, the revenue curve associated with a given level of profit will resemble that shown in Figure 6.5 as the iso-profit revenue curve.

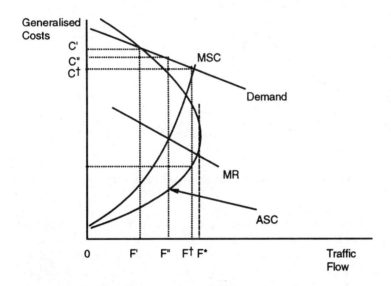

Figure 6.4
The public access problem

The iso-demand contour in the diagram shows a level of demand (in this case the highest attainable with the zero profit revenue curve) consistent with different trips offered/fare combinations. Optimally, T trips will be offered by the transport supplier at a fare of P.

The situation observed before the 1978 Airline Deregulation Act in the US (Douglas and Miller, 1974), however, indicated fares nearer the P* level and trips offered nearer T*. The regulatory system had in effect been captured (Altshuler and Teal, 1979 describe it as 'a system of industry self government') with the result that the size of the industry was sub-optimally large for the market conditions then prevailing.

Those supplying transport services in conditions where rates are regulated to ensure only normal profits are earned will pursue secondary objectives, such as revenue maximisation, and will also have no incentive to combat pressures of factor suppliers (e.g. labour unions, equipment suppliers, etc.) wishing to maximise their sales. The consequences in terms of additional noise, accident risk and fuel wastage are clear. The mechanism leading to this situation in the USA according to Panzar's analysis, represented the indirect capture of the system by the airline labour unions and the airframe manufacturers.

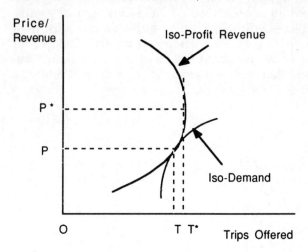

Figure 6.5
The implications of rate-of-return controls with no output limitations

6.3-5 Administrative overlaps.
Administrative structures are important in determining the degree to which regulatory regimes operate effectively. The main problem, as mentioned earlier, is that intervention failures can result from inappropriate and, especially, overlapping administrative responsibilities. Indeed in many countries this problem is typified by the existence of separate Ministries of Transport and Ministries of the Environment that have overlapping responsibilities. A good practical example of this administrative difficulty with overlapping and ultimately uncertain responsibilities relates to the carriage of hazardous materials in the USA (Table 6.4).

This type of problem is not directly an economic issue in the traditional sense other than it does involve both questions of transactions costs and the extent to which economic techniques can assist in optimising the administrative structure. What is clear, however, is that without appropriate administration of regulation both within the environmental sphere and where environmental issues interface with other forms of regulation, then the potential for interventions failing increases.

Table 6.4
Agencies responsible for the transport of hazardous materials in the USA

Responsibility	Regulation of:-									
	Hazardous materials	Containers	Vehicles & vessels	Operators	Planning	Record-keeping	Inspection	Enforcement	Training	Emergency response
DOT:										
RSPA	•	•			•	•	•	•	•	
FHWA		•	•	•	•	•	•	•	•	
FRA		•	•		•	•	•	•	•	
FAA		•	•	•	•	•	•	•	•	
USCG	•	•	•	•	•	•	•	•	•	•
FEMA									•	•
EPA	•				•	•	•	•		•
NRC	•	•			•	•	•	•		•
DOE	•	•			•	•	•	•		•
DOD	•			•	•	•	•	•		•

Key:-

DOT: Department of Transportation
RSPA: Research & Special Programs Administration
FHWA: Federal Highway Administration
FRA: Federal Railroad Administration
FAA: Federal Aviation Administration
USCG: US Coast Guard

FEMA: Federal Emergency Management Agency
EPA: Environmental Protection Agency
NRC: Nuclear Regulatory Commission
DOE: Department of Energy
DOD: Department of Defense

Source: US Congress, Office of Technology Assessment (1986)

6.4 The Problems of Predicting Future Trends

While strictly intervention failures stem from inappropriate actions by governments and regulators brought about when they have access to full information, or at least sufficient relevant information not to make significant mistakes, it is worthwhile spending a little time on pondering the difficulties policy makers have in defining futures. Making mistakes because of inadequate information is inevitable although as discussed later there are ways of containing the problem. Quite well thought-through policies may produce unexpected outcomes because of the inability to predict accurately.

From an environmental policy perspective the predictions of the future are at least as important as the past if for no other reason than to establish some counterfactual against which policy initiatives may be judged. Some general observations seem justified, therefore, highlighting some of the key problems involved in forecasting transport patterns for the future. The aim here is not to produce any type of forecast, although in Chapter 3 we did provide discussion of some of the more important changes that are occurring and their potential future environmental implications, but rather to point briefly to the nature of some of the uncertainties involved. In a way these difficulties themselves suggest the need for flexibility and care in policy formulation as well as for more research to reach a greater understanding of transport and related markets.

First, there is the question of car ownership and use. As our earlier tables have shown (Chapter 2), the motor car is rapidly becoming the dominant mode of passenger transport in the industrialised world. Expert opinion is that this is unlikely to be reversed (Altshuler *et al*, 1984) and the real questions concern the speed at which car ownership and use will rise and whether there is some ultimate saturation level to car use. Regarding the idea that there may be eventual saturation level, the forecasting models used in most countries (irrespective of the detailed specification) implicitly assume a sigmoid growth path for car ownership with initial rapid growth but subsequently with successive additions to the vehicle stock adding marginally less to the total traffic volume (Button *et al*, 1982). They do not, therefore, assume car ownership will go on rising forever. The level of saturation in car ownership employed, however, is important in these calculations (see Figure 6.6) and, for example, somewhat different projects would be obtained using Saturation 1 rather than Saturation 2. There is also the question of how the saturation level is reached - the specification of the growth curve itself.

Second, there is the question of feedback mechanisms. There is a tendency with all forms of forecasting to extrapolate, albeit often in an extremely sophisticated manner, past trends and relationships. In practice there are a variety of ways in which changes in policy stimulate change and reactions which feedback through the system and produce unpredicted outcomes. Individuals confronted with a policy constraint are in effect very adept at finding ways around it which suit them but not always the policy makers.

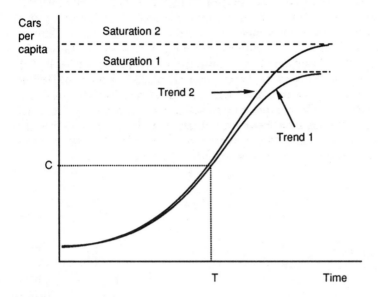

Figure 6.6
Predicting car ownership

In the transport context the main feedbacks are through technology, activity patterns and land use. We have, for instance, very limited abilities to predict with any degree of certainty the long-term impact of raising fuel prices (e.g. through a carbon tax) to reduce the emission of green-house gases. Elasticities exist for short term analysis (e.g. see Goodwin, 1992) but in the longer term industry responds by developing more fuel-efficient cars. Equally, activity patterns are difficult to predict. The introduction of area licensing in Singapore designed to discourage people taking cars into the city during rush hours was thought likely to lead to increased demands on park-and-ride facilities. In fact the greatest impacts have been on car pooling and changes in the timing of trip-making. Finally, despite many years of research we know very little about the interaction of transport and land use. That feedback mechanisms exist seems to be agreed on; how they operate is still rather unclear.

Autonomous technical change, including management practices, poses particular problems in the transport field. New forms of informatics (e.g. electronic data interchange systems) have, for example, influenced both personal and commercial transport activities. Outside of transport, changes in service sector technology and organisation have resulted in new travel-to-work patterns emerging in many cities. Consequently, quite rational policies aimed at reducing environmental degradation in one context may rapidly become outdated as technology alters the overall environment in which transportation is undertaken.

Finally, there are problems in predicting the nature of environmental issues themselves. As more information is gathered so our knowledge about the environment increases. With this greater knowledge come additional problems of defining appropriate trade-offs. Policy makers may have acted very soundly in several countries in the 1970s to tackle some forms of environmental pollution by stimulating the use of diesel engines but now, with increased research this strategy is open to question. On a more macro-scale environmental policies of the 1970s were concerned almost exclusively with local, indeed mainly urban, problems (Foster, 1974) without thought to their implications for global warming or higher-level ozone depletion.

7 Instruments of Economic Policy: Fiscal Tools

7.1 Fiscal Instruments

In any discussion of policies to ameliorate the environmental excesses of transport it is useful at the outset to consider exactly where and in what form fiscal policy, and indeed regulatory measures, may be applied.

Regulations (in their broadest sense) to improve the environment can be introduced at several different points in the chain leading to the final adverse consequences for human welfare. Figure 7.1 provides a simple schema illustrating this.

The environmental problems result from either failures in transport markets or in the existing regulatory framework. (Remedial policy at this stage would require appropriate adjustments to prices, physical regulations, etc.) As we have seen the result of these economic and intervention failures is that the nature of the transport system generated is sub-optimal, often from a purely transport perspective as well as an environmental perspective. (Remedial policies at this level would include such things as traffic management, traffic calming, re-design of vehicles etc.) The outcome of an environmentally sub-optimal transport system manifests itself in the form of atmospheric pollution, noise, etc. as outlined above. (Remedial actions here would involve regulations involving compulsory end-of-pipeline treatment such as the use of silencers, the fitting of catalytic converters, specifications on bumper fitting and design, etc.) Finally, there are the actual effects on human welfare. (Regulations at this stage would include such things as compensation laws, provision of screening from traffic noise, etc.)

Theoretically, it is often argued that ideally one should tackle transport-related environmental problems at source, i.e. at the causes stage. There are, however, good reasons why this is not always the best option. The entwined nature of economic systems coupled with the need to prioritise objectives may make it difficult to develop strategies which reduce environmental difficulties without simultaneously making it difficult to meet other objectives such as: fostering economic growth, ensuring acceptable regional economic disparities, meeting defence priorities, etc.

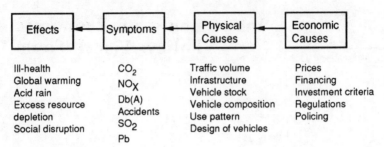

Effects	Symptoms	Physical Causes	Economic Causes
Ill-health	CO_2	Traffic volume	Prices
Global warming	NO_X	Infrastructure	Financing
Acid rain		Vehicle stock	Investment criteria
Excess resource	Db(A)	Vehicle composition	Regulations
depletion	Accidents	Use pattern	Policing
Social disruption	SO_2	Design of vehicles	
	Pb		

Figure 7.1
The links between economic policies on urban transport and the environment

Second, there are transactions costs involved in policing, monitoring and modifying economic policies and because of these in many cases it may be more efficient not to try and resolve the underlying economic problem but to, say introduce some end-of-pipeline treatment or to instigate compulsory compensation schemes.

Finally, there are issues of political reality to be addressed. Quite simply given the political situations in many countries and the coalitions of interests which exist, it has proved more practical in many cases to seek to reduce the environmental damage caused by transport through measures towards the end of the chain set out in Figure 7.1 rather than to try to remedy the root economic causes. Here, however, we seek to explore fiscal reforms, in the form of appropriate taxes, charges, subsidies etc., which could tackle transport-related environmental problems at source.

It is perhaps useful at the outset to give some idea of the types of instrument which we are concerned with and to set them into some sort of context. If we focus exclusively on the environmental problems of the motor car then a simple taxonomy of possible policy instruments is set out in Table 7.1. It should be said that the list is not intended to be comprehensive but rather illustrative. It also contains examples of command-and-control instruments - the subject of the next chapter - for comparative purposes.

The key points are, firstly, that it is often useful to think in terms of direct and indirect instruments. This is not strictly related to the links set out in Table 7.1 but there are overlaps. Direct instruments, which are rather limited in their number and are, in fact, seldom actually adopted by policy makers for reasons discussed in Chapter 9, essentially try to tackle the underlying market or intervention failures. The indirect instruments act upon the other stages set out in Table 7.1 and impact more on the ways cars are used and the nature of the inputs employed rather than upon environmental intrusion *per se*. While we do not rigidly follow this taxonomy in our discussions, and we

Table 7.1
Taxonomy of policy instruments to control the environmental impacts of motor vehicles

	Market based incentives		Command and control regulations	
	Direct	Indirect	Direct	Indirect
Vehicle	•Emissions fees	•Tradable permits •Differential vehicle taxation •Tax allowances for new vehicles	•Emissions standards	•Compulsory inspection and maintenance of emissions control systems •Mandatory use of low polluting vehicles •Compulsory scrappage of old vehicles
Fuel		•Differential fuel taxation •High fuel taxes	•Fuel composition •Phasing out of high polluting fuels	•Fuel economy standards •Speed limits
Traffic		•Congestion charges •Parking charges •Subsidies for less polluting modes	•Physical restraint of traffic •designated routes	•Restraints on vehicle use Bus lanes and other priorities

Source: Cabajo (1991)

also tend to add to the list of instruments that Cabajo set down in his table, it does form the basis for the ordering of material in this and the following chapter; direct and indirect fiscal and command-and-control measures are looked at in turn.

7.2 Emissions Charges

Since the publication of Pigou's (1920) seminal work a large number of economists have expended considerable energies in arguing the merits for adopting emissions charges. These essentially involve the authorities taking responsibility for the environment and charging users of the environment an appropriate price (or tax) for that use. The general rationale for doing this was recently clearly expressed in the *Blueprint for a Green Economy* (Pearce *et al*, 1989):

> ....the economic principles underlying the *proper* pricing of goods and services and of natural resources are the same. Prices should reflect the true social costs of production and use. Essentially this means getting the true values of environmental services reflected in prices, rather than having them treated as 'free goods'.

Figure 7.2 provides an illustration of how such a charge would apply to transport. Without the internalisation of the external costs of traffic, let us say the noise of aircraft operating at an airport near a residential area, the traffic level would be at Q - the level which maximises the net private benefit to those using the airport. This clearly exceeds the socially optimal traffic level Q*. To reduce traffic to this optimum a tax of t per unit of traffic would need to be imposed. This makes the aircraft operators aware of their social costs and stimulates them to treat (MNPB-t) as their relevant decision-making parameter.

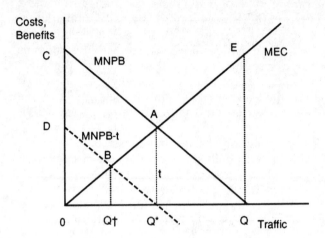

Figure 7.2
The idea of the Pigouvian Tax

Now while the basic concept is not difficult to appreciate it has been refined and argued over for the past seventy years. This is not the place for a blow-by-blow account of the theoretical debates (Baumol and Oates, 1988, have some discussion of this) but one or two points are worth highlighting.

Perhaps the most important of these is the fact that it is the authorities who impose the Pigouvian tax who are the main beneficiaries. The airlines in our example lose. Those affected by the noise gain by some reduction in its level but are not freed entirely from it. The problem is outlined in Buchanan and Stubblebine (1962). The authorities gain revenues of CDAQ* by imposing the charge and the airlines suffer both this loss in terms of payments of the charge and the MNPB previously enjoyed from the Q*Q landings they no longer find viable i.e. a loss of Q*AQ. From the residents' perspective, while the tax in Figure 7.2 will reduce activities to the level Q*, and thus benefit them by QEAQ*, they will still have to endure noise nuisance which is equal, in welfare terms, to OAQ*. This latter fact, according to Buchanan and Stubblebine, means that Q* is not a stable equilibrium - essentially for traffic levels between Q* and Q† the noise nuisance which remains exceeds the after-tax value to the airlines of their activities at the airport. If bargaining were possible then this would in fact take place with a resultant equilibrium at Q† landings.

While interesting, how relevant this type of argument is in practice is questionable. In particular, it seems to assume that Coasian trading is not possible initially, and thus government intervention is required, but then assumes that once a Pigouvian tax is in place bargaining becomes a reality. One cannot think of many cases in a transport context where this is likely. It also applies rather more to small-number situations where a limited number of victims have the ability to influence the level of tax (e.g. by firms moving noise-sensitive activities such as some forms of electronics production) and thus push up the MEC curve and the tax. Resultant bargaining would benefit them. Such cases seem rather rare in the transport field and, if they do occur, the Coasian solution is to put a tax on victims to discourage such activities.

While hardly common, pollution charges have been used in transport with some success. One clear illustration of where fiscal incentives (in this example, coupled with regulation) have proved particularly effective has been in reducing the levels of lead (Pb) pollution. Many countries have introduced significant tax differentials between leaded and unleaded gasoline (see Table 7.2) but equally many have also initiated regulations regarding the fuels which can be sold. In particular, the banning of normal gasoline (providing the tank capacity for garages to stock unleaded fuel and leaving only the more expensive super) has effectively further reduced the real choice open to most automobile users in the Netherlands, Switzerland, the UK and Germany. The combined impact of these measures in the UK was a rise in vehicles using unleaded gasoline from 0.1 percent of the car park in March 1988 to 25.9 percent in October 1989. Similarly, in the pre-unified FRG the percentage of automobiles using unleaded rose from 11 percent in 1986 to 28 percent in 1987.

Table 7.2
VAT and excise duty (in ECU per thousand litres) on petrol and diesel fuels in EC Members as of 1 January 1990

| | Leaded Petrol | | Unleaded petrol | | Diesel | |
	VAT(%)	Duty	VAT(%)	Duty	VAT(%)	Duty
Belgium	25.0	325	25.0	291	25.0	190.0
Denmark	22.0	424	22.0	343	22.0	223.0
Germany	14.0	321	14.0	281	14.0	218.0
Greece	36.0	198	36.0	152	6.0	4.0
Spain	12.0	331	12.0	316	12.0	190.0
France	18.6	448	18.6	397	18.6	231.0
Ireland	25.0	395	25.0	373	25.0	290.0
Italy	19.0	580	19.0	538	19.0	279.0
Luxembourg	12.0	234	6.0	140	12.0	101.0
Netherlands	18.5	346	18.5	342	18.5	158.0
Portugal	8.0	424	8.0	380	8.0	213.0
UK	15.0	277	15.0	240	15.0	234.0

A further illustration, albeit of a somewhat different type, of the impact of charging relates to diesel fuels. In Europe, as can be seen from Table 7.2, there is a general tax differential in favour of diesel fuel. In the past, especially prior to the adoption of unleaded gasoline and the introduction of the catalytic converter this incentive to use diesel was justified in part by the greater fuel efficiency of such engines and their lower emissions of such pollutants as carbon monoxide, nitrogen oxide and hydrocarbons.

It is in Italy where the impact of differential taxation has had the greatest effect with nearly 7 percent of the total number of automobiles and some 22 percent of the total new car sales in 1983 being diesel. The duty on diesel fuel in Italy during 1987 represented only 55.6 percent of retail price compared with a duty of 78.6 percent on gasoline. One should perhaps note that until recently there has been a zero penetration of diesel automobiles in the Greek market, despite a significant positive gasoline-diesel fuel price differential. This can, however, be explained by a total prohibition on their use.

The diesel tax example provides a useful illustration of one of the problems with using charges. Unlike the lead example, the differential diesel tax is not strictly a charge on emissions but rather a charge aimed at the physical causes of pollution associated with gasoline use. It obviously has an impact in terms of which fuels are used but its importance in an environmental context is unclear because of the complex cocktail of chemicals produced in the burning of all fuels. Standard diesel engines emit about 10 percent of the carbon monoxide and hydrocarbons emitted by conventional gasoline engines and 65 percent of the nitrogen oxides. They are also very efficient in terms of fuel consumption. However, advances in the technology of the internal combustion engine coupled with catalytic converters remove these advantages. Moreover, diesel engines generate more smoke, toxic particulates and polyaromatic hydrocarbons, which are both toxic and possibly carcinogenic. Diesel engines also adversely affect the local environment in that they are generally noisy; technical advances are reducing this problem on existing types of vehicles but future direct injection engines are potentially noisier. What one is doing in this case, therefore, is taxing to favour a particular package of environmental effects rather than targeting specific emissions and charging for their adverse impacts.

7.3   Tradeable (Marketable) Permits

Although the emissions charges have an established pedigree in economic theory, their widespread adoption has tended to be rather limited because of a lack of political confidence that they can achieve desired environmental and other targets - a point we return to in Chapter 9. One method advocated to circumvent this problem and to ensure that targets are attained at minimum cost is to adopt systems of tradeable (or marketable) permits.

The idea has its origin in the pollution rights concept. Under a tradeable permits system these rights are allocated by the authorities but, once obtained, can be traded. Thus, the environment is turned into a tradeable commodity and those consuming the environment have an incentive to adopt more efficient technologies. The important point is that the overall level of environmental encroachment can be contained by limiting the number of permits but, in turn, the trading which is then permitted means that this environmental consumption is internalised within the cost functions of firms. Some people see them as a more acceptable means of handling pollution than charges because they avoid certain administrative difficulties, e.g.,

> A major advantage of the marketable permit approach is that it gives the environmental authority direct control over the quantity of emissions. Under the fees approach, the regulator must set a fee, and if, for example, the fee turns out to be too low, pollution will exceed permissible levels. The agency will find itself in the uncomfortable position of having to adjust and readjust the fee to ensure that the environmental standard is attained. Direct control over quantity is to be preferred since the standard itself is prescribed in quantity terms. (Cropper and Oates, 1992)

The key points concerning tradeable permits are illustrated in Figure 7.3. We assume that a permit is required for each unit of pollution generated and that the number of permits issued are recorded on the horizontal. The marginal abatement cost (MAC) and marginal externality cost (MEC) curves are assumed to take the standard form. The optimal number of permits to be issued in this case is Q^t, which also indicates the optimal level of pollution, and the permit supply schedule is shown as S^t. With trading permitted, the resultant market price for a permit will be P^t.

It is important to note that under this type of regime the MAC curve becomes the demand curve for permits, a point easily seen if one considers that at any price above P^t the number of permits demand will fall because it is financially cheaper to clean up production. This fact is helpful because it means that MAC must also represent the horizontal summation of the MAC curves of the individual firms in the market. Suppose we have two firms with associated marginal abatement cost curves of MAC_1 and MAC_2 respectively. With the market price for permits at P^t, this means they will buy Q_1 and Q_2 permits respectively. Assuming an initially equal allocation of permits, the high cost of abatement producer will, in consequence, buy permits and the low cost of abatement supply will sell them. In terms of long-term impacts this will stimulate a shift to low cost of abatement technology but smooth transition as higher-cost producers can, albeit at the cost of buying emissions permits, continue production in the short term.

Although not marketable in the strict sense that there exists a free-market situation, tradeable permits offer some scope for enhancing efficiency. They have mainly been used in the US and also mainly in the context of static sources of pollution. The 1970 Clean Air Act estab-

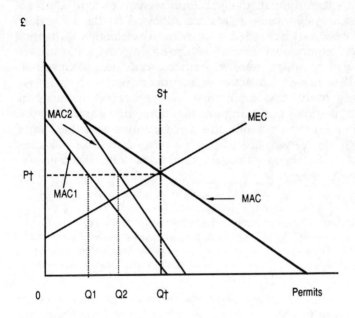

Figure 7.3
The outcome using marketable permits

lished national Ambient Air Quality Standards to be controlled by the Environmental Protection Agency (EPA). As it transpired, by the mid-1970s it became clear that many of the states were not achieving their State Implementation Plan targets. In consequence a series of measures designed to both increase flexibility in the system and also to contain implementation costs were initiated from 1974 (Hahn and Hester, 1989; Liroff, 1986). Initially, some degree of internal trading was permitted within undertakings whereby firms, in the process of technical change, could increase emissions from new sources if they reduced them from other, existing sources. In 1979, external trading became possible as bubbles were introduced. These cover several sources of existing pollution, possibly at a number of plants, and permit the producers to trade-off their respective emissions provided the prescribed limit is not exceeded.

The effects of tradeable permits on transport are at best indirect in that they have acted to reduce the environmental damage associated with manufacturing the hardware of the sector (i.e. automobiles, rail wagons, etc.). There are, however, some more explicit examples such as the Corporate Average Fuel Economy Standards (CAFE) introduced in the USA during 1975. These were designed to reduce gasoline consumption by causing manufacturers to improve the fuel economy of their vehicles. Certain standards - 18 miles per gallon by 1978 and 27.5 miles per gallon by 1985 - were set and the harmonic average fuel consumption of a manufacturer's fleet was to conform to these. By not stipulating the efficiency of different weight and engine sizes this theoretically allowed manufacturers to improve the fuel efficiency of those types of vehicle where this was most economical.

More explicit use of marketable rights in the context of transport can be seen in the USA's lead trading programme which introduced a system of lead credits for a pre-defined five-year period from 1982. The standard was gradually reduced from 1.1 grams/gallon for large refineries in 1982 to 0.1 grams/gallon for all refineries in 1986. Further, while initially refineries were not permitted to bank permits for future use or sale, banking was allowed three years into the regime. The programme was aimed at allowing gasoline refineries greater flexibility during a period when lead in gasoline was being reduced. The initial allocation of credits was based on existing production levels and trading of the credits was very high - about 15 percent of the lead used in 1985 was traded. While no *ex post* estimates of the financial advantages of the system over rigid lead allocations to refineries are available, the Environmental Protection Agency forecast savings of about $228 million in 1985 but this seems to have been exceeded (Hahn and Hester, 1989). At the same time it seems to have had the same impact on environmental quality as would a rigid non-tradeable regime.

One can, however, envisage further systems whereby on type approval a motor vehicle would be allocated to an emissions class, and the manufacturer would purchase an emissions certificate for each vehicle which, in turn, he sells to the vehicle's purchaser. If then the owner retro-fits environmentally beneficial technologies then he can sell his certificate and buy a cheaper one relevant to the new class his vehicle falls into (Rothengatter, 1989).

7.4 The Case for Road Pricing

Automobile users and commercial vehicle operators pay a wide variety of charges to use the road network. While the ratios and levels differ between countries, most road users in industrial countries are subjected to annual licence fees (a sort of club membership) and fuel taxes together with local charges for parking and tolls on some elements of the road network. There is thus a price for using roads although this is not what economists generally understand by the term 'road pricing'. In particular, the charges levied on road users relate very little to the costs of providing and maintaining the infrastructure provided let alone to wider notions of optimising its use either from a purely traffic perspective or from a much wider social perspective (Newbery, 1988; Small *et al*, 1989). The point has been firmly made some time ago by Vickrey (1963):

> I will begin with the proposition that in no other major area are pricing practices so irrational, so out of date, and so conducive to waste as in urban trans-

portation. Two aspects are particularly deficient: the absence of adequate peak-off-peak differentials and the gross underpricing of some modes relative to others. In nearly all other operations characterised by peak load problems, at least some attempt is made to differentiate between the rates charged for peak and for off-peak services. Where competition exists, this pattern is enforced by competition: resort hotels have off-peak rates; theatres charge more at weekends and less for matinees. Telephone calls are cheaper at night ..... But in transportation, such differentiation as exists is usually perverse.

There is often some confusion as to what exactly road pricing entails. It is sometimes interpreted as charging so as to optimise road use but, in fact, it tends to take on a more specific meaning in economics. One often reads, for instance, of it involving charging road users for the marginal social costs of their trips but even this is too broad. Road pricing involves charging the road user only for the full marginal costs of trips as they affect other road users - society is thus being rather narrowly defined. In simple terms it is a means of making urban road users aware of the congestion costs they impose on other road users and thus make effective use of a road network from a transport management perspective.

Although road pricing is not strictly a mechanism for handling environmental costs it does impact on one of the underlying causes of these excessive degradations, namely sub-optimal traffic volumes. Figure 7.4 sets down the economic case for road pricing. We are dealing here with the most basic case involving a single road being used by a number of identical motorists. (Of course, there may be interactions between traffic flows on different links in a road network or there may be bottlenecks on the route - these factors complicate, but do not devalue, the framework.) Further, we assume there are q vehicles on the road, spaced evenly over a time period - say an hour. Each vehicle takes D/v hours (the distance divided by speed) to travel the road at a travel cost (variable vehicle running costs plus time costs) of c per hour. Hence the cost to one driver of reaching his destination is $c(\partial/v)$. For ease of exposition we assume the road is a mile long (i.e. D=1) so that the average cost of travel reduces to £c/v per mile with a total cost for all vehicles of TC = (qc)/v. The marginal cost of each additional vehicle is thus:

$$MC = \frac{\partial TC}{\partial q} = \frac{c}{v} - \left\{ \frac{qc\partial v}{v^2 \partial q} \right\}$$

$$= \frac{vc - qc(\partial v/\partial q)}{v^2}$$

The traveller, however, will only experience the AC (or c/v) since he takes no account of the impedance his activities impose on others. The difference between the AC (or more generally when congestion develops in a more complex network context, the marginal private cost) and the MC is the amount motorists need to be charged to make them cognisant of the full costs of their actions. This optimal road price, r, is defined as:-

$$r = \frac{qc(\partial v/\partial q)}{v^2}$$

Imposing the optimal road price, therefore, reduces traffic flow in the figure by X and maximises the efficiency of use made of the road by motorists. (For more sophisticated analysis see, Walters, 1961; Beesley, 1964.)

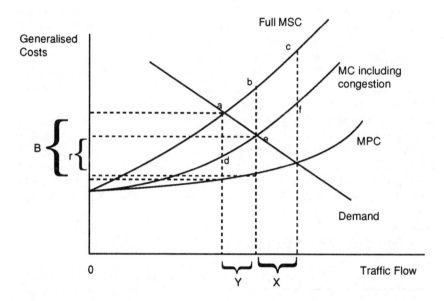

Figure 7.4
The optimum road price

This does not, however, mean that traffic flows are optimised from a wider perspective taking into account environmental costs. If we include these, and make the assumption that they rise more than in proportion to the traffic flow because of various synergy effects, then the optimum traffic flow should fall by a further Y vehicles per hour. A full pricing mechanism embracing all costs would, therefore, require a charge of B over and above the marginal private cost borne by road users. This is higher than the road price as economists understand the term. What road pricing does, therefore, is to reduce the environmental costs of urban road use by an amount equal to area bcfe in Figure 7.4. Optimally, a full charge approach embracing all forms of external, including environmental, costs would mean a further saving in environmental costs equal in money terms to the area abed.

Of course, the figure paints a very simplified picture of the links between private, congestion and environmental costs. While in many instances there is a positive correlation of the general form depicted, the relationship can be more complicated and in some very rare instances it is possible that road pricing could, in cases where congestion is inversely correlated with environmental degradation, lead to an overall diminution of the state of the environment - a point we return to below.

The conventional argument suggesting that excess congestion leads to excessive environmental damage stems to a large degree from the link between congestion and energy use (Transnet, 1990). Congestion impedes the free flow of traffic and this in turn leads to inefficiency in the combustion of fuels. Frequent acceleration and deceleration in particular lead to higher fuel consumption (Table 7.3). This is because not only is more fuel burned for a given journey length, with adverse implications for CO_2 emissions and other atmospheric pollutants, because of the frequency of stopping and starting, but the engines themselves burn that fuel less efficiently quite simply because of the lower average speeds which result and this compounds the levels of atmospheric pollution (Table 7.4). Equally, continual stopping and starting of traffic generates more noise than a smooth traffic flow and the wear and tear on tyres and brakes puts more particulates into the atmosphere. Further, few people find a congested traffic stream aesthetically pleasing and it impedes pedestrian and cycle movements.

Table 7.3
The impacts of acceleration and deceleration on atmospheric pollution

| Pollutants | Composition of exhaust gases (parts per million) | | | |
	Idling	Accelerating	Cruising	Decelerating
Gasoline engines				
Carbon monoxide	69,000	29,000	27,000	39,000
Hydrocarbons	5,300	1,600	1,000	10,000
Nitrogen oxides	30	1,020	650	20
Aldehydes	30	20	10	290
Diesel engines				
Carbon monoxide	trace	1,000	trace	trace
Hydrocarbons	400	200	100	300
Nitrogen oxides	60	350	240	30
Aldehydes	10	20	10	30

Source: Organisation for Economic Cooperation and Development (1983)

Table 7.4
The impact of traffic speed on pollution

| Miles per hour | Emissions (grams per mile) | | |
	Carbon monoxide	Hydrocarbons	Nitrogen oxides
25	55.47	8.75	5.13
40	37.24	7.07	5.85
55	31.66	6.30	6.85

Source: McConnell and Straszheim (1982)

Deriving an overall figure for the total social, including environmental, costs of congestion is almost impossible not only because of the difficulties of putting monetary values on many items involved but also because of the diversity of the elements involved and the specifically local nature of many of their impacts. Khisty and Kaftanski (1986) by making some very strong assumptions and combining rather diverse data sources do suggest, however, that in the USA in 1982 prices the major environmental costs of urban transport are over twice those of the congestion externalities road users impose on each other (Table 7.5).

Table 7.5
The social costs of urban traffic congestion in the USA

Social costs	Cost per vehicle mile (1982 prices)
Travel time	$0.1152
Air pollution	$0.0256
Noise pollution	$0.0037
Excess fuel consumption	$0.1105
Traffic accidents	$0.1265
Total	$0.3815

Source: Khisty and Kaftanski (1986)

Aggregate studies must, however, be treated with caution. There are situations, for instance, when road pricing by lengthening trips or redirecting them to environmentally sensitive residential areas could actually harm the environment. If, for example, road pricing were introduced in one city but not in competing centres this could encourage traffic to redistribute to the latter resulting in lengthier journeys and higher levels of atmospheric pollution. It has also been demonstrated by Goldstein and Moses (1975) that fiscal constraints such as road pricing can, in certain conditions and with certain patterns of land use, lead to the physical spreading out of urban areas with potentially adverse consequences of things such as urban sprawl.

At the more micro-level, some simple forms of road pricing, particularly those involving cordons or area licences, are likely to redistribute traffic to free routes which may pass through residential zones or other areas more sensitive to noise nuisance and other third party effects of traffic than those in central urban areas where the road price is applied. Equally, spreading commuter peaks, which road pricing may well do, could lead to greater traffic volumes at times of the day, such as the early morning and early evening, when previously local environmental impacts were negligible. Care must be taken, therefore, to ensure that a full picture of the total environmental impacts of any electronic road pricing scheme on an urban area is painted prior to its implementation.

The academic literature on road pricing is extensive and growing (see Table 7.6 for a summary of the results of major-desk top studies and the survey by Morrison, 1986) but actual experiences of its application in western cities are limited (e.g. Button, 1984). Also, what has been attempted has tended to involve rather crude technology. These simple schemes involve such things as area licensing whereby a permit must be purchased to take a vehicle into an urban area during peak traffic periods and cordon pricing whereby a fee must be paid as one crosses a boundary into a congested urban area.

Table 7.6
Summary of results from major desk-top studies of road pricing

Study	Place	Road price at peak time (current prices)
Walters (1961)	Generic U.S. Urban Expressway	$0.10-0.15/auto-mile
U.K. Ministry of Transport (1963)	Urban Areas in Great Britain	9d (old pence)/auto-mile
Greater London Council (1974)	Central London	£0.60/auto-day
Elliott (1975)	Los Angeles	$0.03-0.15/auto-mile
Kraus et al (1976)	Twin-Cities Expressways, 1970	$0.03-0.15/auto-mile
Keeler and Small (1977)	Bay Area Expressways, 1972	$0.027-0.343/auto-mile
Dewees (1978)	Toronto, 1973	$0.04-0.38/auto-mile
Cheslow (1978)	Berkeley, 1977	$2.0/auto-trip
Spielberg (1978)	Madison, 1977	$1.0/auto-trip
Mohring (1979)	Twin-Cities	$0.66/auto-mile
Gomez-Ibanez and Fauth (1980)	Boston, 1975	$0.5-1.0/auto-mile
Viton (1980)	Bay Area Bridges, 1972	$0.154/auto-mile
Starrs and Starkie (1986)	Adelaide Arterial Roads 1982	A$0.025-0.22/auto-km
Cameron (1991)	Los Angeles Expressways	$0.15/auto-mile

Source: Derived from Button (1984) and Morrison (1986)

The most extensive experience we have is the area licensing scheme initiated in Singapore in 1975 whereby most vehicles entering the city centre during the morning peak must have a supplementary licence. This is very well documented and the data set out in Table 7.7 provide some basic information on the traffic effects of the scheme. There have been lessons learned over time which have led to modifications in the details of the scheme (e.g. the fee licence charged and the hours of operation) but in the short term it reduced peak traffic considerable and in the longer term kept traffic growth during the peak well below that which had been forecast in the absence of road pricing. Although part of this was due to supplementary measures of high vehicle taxation and the construction of new ring routes, the overall impact on traffic congestion was unquestionably to reduce it considerably (Behbehani *et al*, 1984).

Table 7.7
The traffic effects of the Singapore Area Licensing Scheme

Time	Traffic March 1975	Traffic May 1976	Traffic May 1979	Traffic May 1983
Cars				
07.00-07.30	5,384	5,675	5,723	6,413
07.30-10.15	42,790	10,754	13,181	15,473
10.15-10.45	na	6,459	5,527	7,069
All vehicles				
07.00-07.30	9,800	10,332	10,596	11,280
07.30-10.15	74,014	35,787	49,606	57,035
10.15-10.45	na	13,441	15,179	16,490

Source: Behbehani *et al* (1984)

In terms of the wider environmental impacts of the scheme, the evidence is that in the period between 1976 and 1982 there was a rise in CO_2 concentrations in the centre of Singapore which reflected the overall growth in traffic over the period. Road pricing may have acted to limit this. Total acidity in the atmosphere, smoke levels and nitric oxides and dioxides, however, fell significantly although how much of this was due to area licensing and how much to other elements of transport policy and industrial policy is impossible to discover. Evidence on noise pollution is unavailable but the number of all types of accident, despite higher overall traffic volumes, decreased over the period.

Cordon charges, although still far from widespread, are becoming increasingly common with Bergen and Oslo being the most obvious examples. The motivation in most cases, however, is not strictly that of directly containing congestion but rather of revenue raising for infrastructure building. Indeed, in the case of Oslo, the stated objective is not to reduce traffic but explicitly to raise revenue to finance major road and other transport projects in Oslo and the surrounding county district of Akershus.

Since a charge is levied in cordon schemes, however, it is almost inevitable that there will be some impact on travel behaviour and *ipso facto* they may have positive environmental implication. In some instances, such as Oslo (Solheim, 1990), an argument has also been advanced that since the revenue collected is to be used to construct ring road facilities, which in turn will ultimately reduce congestion and take traffic away from environmentally sensitive areas, and to a lesser extent (some 10 percent of revenue) fund public transport, there will be long-term positive secondary local environmental gains.

Certainly, the indications from the scheme initiated in Bergen in 1986 (Larsen, 1988) are that cordons do impact in traffic flows crossing them. The Bergen scheme covers the period 06.00 to 22.00 hours each weekday, and consequently is not just confined to congested periods of the day, but it has induced a 6 to 7 percent reduction in car traffic in the urban area (see Table 7.8). In the case of Oslo, which again initially had a fixed level of charge throughout the day, there was a small initial fall in the level of traffic crossing the cordon after the introduction of charges in 1990 but within nine months the flows were more or less back to normal (Solheim, 1990). The detailed implications for the environment have not, however, been explored in either case.

Table 7.8
The impact of the Bergen Toll Ring

Time period	Percentage change in the number of trips	
	Cars with Seasonal Pass	Cars Paying per Trip
Monday-Friday		
0600-0900	-0.3	-40.8
0900-1700	12.2	-21.1
1700-2200	2.1	-35.2
Toll Period Total	5.4	-29.8

Source: Larson (1988)

There are two broad ways of implementing more sophisticated forms of electronic road pricing. The first uses automatic vehicle identification (AVI), which records centrally the congestion costs of individual trips for each vehicle. The second does not identify individual vehicles but deducts the cost of using congested roads from a stored value medium (similar to the current use of telephone cards) where the proprietor of the system is not able to establish who is using the facility (Thompson, 1990). This latter approach, which might usefully be called non-smart card technology, can be extended to the use of smart cards, similar to credit cards, which automatically debits the costs of trips directly from bank accounts or charges them to a credit card account (such as VISA).

There is very little practical experience of electronic road pricing. There has been experimentation with equipment and operational practices in Hong Kong (Dawson and Catling, 1986) and various forms of AVI systems have been devised and tested essentially as a means of collecting tolls (Hensher, 1991). On the operational side, the two-year experiment of electronic road pricing in Hong Kong during the mid-1980s involved fitting over 2,500 vehicles with AVIs together with the setting of electronic loops in the road surface at the edge of charge zones. When a vehicle crossed a boundary, a power loop energised its AVI which in turn sent a message, via inductive receiver loops, to a road side recorder. What it did was to give some credence to the view expressed in the Smeed Report that metering devices could be 'developed into an efficient charging system' (UK Ministry of Transport, 1964). The technical and economic feasibility of the electronic road pricing system used was found to have achieved 99 percent effectiveness and reliability against the criteria set it.

There are, however, practical difficulties with the Hong Kong style of road pricing, especially in terms of devising a mechanism enabling its phased introduction on a large scale and of road users having a poor idea of the road price they must pay in advance of making a trip. Many now argue that non-smart and smart card types of systems may prove more viable (Thompson, 1990).

The Netherlands has been particularly forward in advocating the adoption of such systems and recently, although now postponed, plans were drawn up to have electronic road pricing based on this technology operational in the west of the Netherlands (the Randstad) by the mid-1990s (Netherlands Ministry of Transport and Public Works, 1989). The objectives were partly environmental as set out in the Second Transport Structure Plan and explicitly aimed at reducing the growth of car traffic. Political factors, however, watered down the extent to which electronic road pricing will actually be deployed and the plan has become little more than a scheme for automatic tolling for tunnels. Interest in electronic road pricing also has a long history in the UK and there is the possibility that Cambridge will adopt a form of it to combat its severe traffic congestion problems. The system proposed (Pease, 1990) employs dedicated, non-smart cards from which the road-user charge is deducted.

Despite the interest being shown in adopting road pricing little detailed work has been conducted on the potential environmental implications of the schemes. One exception involves desk-top studies carried out in Stockholm. While initial enthusiasm for road pricing has recently waned somewhat in Stockholm, and plans put forward in the late 1980s to initiate electronic road pricing have been pushed back, detailed analysis of policy options have been conducted (Ramjerdi, 1989). These simulation studies indicated that a cordon style of road pricing involving a 25SK per car fee for a round trip would not only considerably increase traffic speeds in the controlled area but also reduce NO_x emissions by 12 percent and CO emissions by 73 percent.

Before leaving the topic of road pricing it is worth saying a few words about the use of parking policy as an urban traffic policy instrument. Parking policy acts as a complement to urban road use. Even if there was road pricing there would be a need for an optimal parking pricing policy both to allocate existing spaces efficiently in the short run and to provide guidelines as to the need for investment in

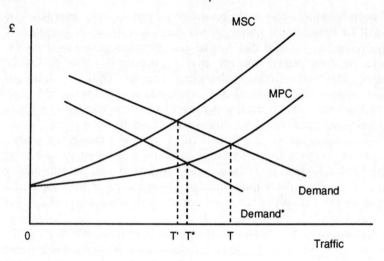

Figure 7.5
The effects of parking charges

capacity in the long run. Here we are talking about something beyond this.

Pushing up the price of parking, by imposing charges specifically aimed at deterring traffic beyond the level justified simply for allocating parking spaces *per se*, will shift the demand curve for road use to the left (i.e. from Demand to Demand* in Figure 7.5). The policy could result in an optimal flow (i.e. T') but is more likely to yield improvements rather than an optimal outcome (i.e. result in some traffic flow such as T*). There are also distribution complexities with terminal policies of this type which affect the composition of traffic. They penalise stopping traffic but benefit and, indeed, can encourage through traffic which is in a position to make use of less congested streets at no additional cost (Glazer and Niskanen, 1992). They also have spatial distribution implications in that longer-distance terminating traffic has a relatively smaller burden to bear than does shorter distance traffic. How to regulate the costs of using privately supplied parking facilities poses additional problems. The need to zone parking charge areas also means that spatial (as well as temporal) sensitivity is poor. Indeed, such zoning is likely to induce fringe parking effects around the borders of zones (Gillen, 1978).

Despite these problems, parking charges have for many years been regulated in a large number of cities in part to discourage the use of cars for commuting and shopping purposes. The attention given to the policy has not diminished over time and, indeed, in 1990 Mayor Bradley of Los Angeles proposed parking fees as a substitute for road-user fees. The congestion-reducing impact of increasing public parking fees has in practice, however, tended to be mixed.

In a study of nine US cities, Kuzmyak and Schreffler (1990) found that parking fees and restrictions were the most effective component of the traffic management schemes adopted. But the impact of such policies is often less than was hoped for. One reason for the rather limp response to high parking fees found in some cities is that many commuters who contribute to rush-hour congestion park free - e.g. in the US Willson and Shoup (1990) estimated that 90 percent of US car commuters park free at work. Further, many parking places are private off-street facilities (e.g. up to 60 percent in UK cities such as Bristol, Oxford, Cambridge, etc.) which makes the direct imposition of high parking fees difficult. This need to deal with private parking if terminal fees are to be an alternative to road pricing has recently come to the fore in New Zealand where the Parliamentary Commission on the Environment has recommended as an anti-congestion measure that employees pay a tax on free parking provided by employers.

Even public parking, and especially on-street parking, policy has seldom been as effective as advocates have hoped. While low enforcement costs and public acceptance have been voiced as specific merits of parking charges there is limited evidence to support such views. The evidence that we do have from countries such as Italy (Ponti and Vittadini, 1990) and the Netherlands (Nijkamp *et al*, 1990) is that such systems are variable in terms of their efficiency in limiting congestion. There is little evidence of public acceptance of high parking fees and they tend to be evaded except in the face of heavy policing and, *ipso facto*, transactions costs. This is, for example, borne out in the London situation where tightening of policing of traffic regulations, including parking policies, on 'Red Routes' was a key element leading to reduced congestion on designated traffic corridors but the policing costs have been high in terms of the commitment of necessary manpower.

7.5   Fuel Taxation and Licence Fees

Most forms of transport are subject to taxation - either on an annual or usage basis. In particular, fuel is taxed and in most countries vehicles are subject to licence fees. The historical reasons for such taxation lie mainly in the need to raise sumptuary revenues. They can form, and indeed have formed, in some instances the basis of indirect fiscal instruments for environmental policy. They are generally seen as rather blunt instruments in this latter role but the fact that they are already in place means that it is often politically expedient to adapt them in the best way possible rather than seek legislation for new, probably more effective, alternatives.

The use of high fuel charges has been advocated by some as a tractable and politically acceptable means of controlling congestion even by those who see road pricing as a considerably superior policy instrument (e.g. Mohring, 1989). There is evidence of some degree of sensitivity in vehicle efficiency to the price of fuel (Table 7.9) but, of course, this does not mean all forms of environmental damage are reduced. Several countries, however, do use fuel taxation policy to combat congestion. Singapore, for example, which has a 50 percent fuel tax, is the most obvious. Detailed analysis of the specific impact of such policies on congestion is lacking but overall the evidence tends to show that the long-run fuel price elasticity of demand for car use is low. A recent survey by Goodwin, for example, produced the elasticities of traffic levels with respect to petrol price shown in Table 7.10.

Table 7.9
Impact of gasoline prices on fuel efficiency in the USA

Year	City	Miles per US Gallon Highway	Harmonic mean	Real price of gasoline (1967=100)
1968	12.59	18.42	14.69	97.3
1969	12.60	18.62	14.74	95.4
1970	12.59	19.01	14.85	90.8
1971	12.27	18.18	14.37	87.6
1972	12.15	18.90	14.48	85.9
1973	12.01	18.07	14.15	88.7
1974	12.03	18.23	14.21	108.3
1975	13.68	19.45	15.79	106.0
1976	15.23	21.27	17.46	105.3
1977	15.99	22.26	18.31	103.7
1978	17.24	24.48	19.89	100.5
1979	17.70	24.60	20.25	122.2
1980	20.35	29.02	23.51	149.6
1981	21.75	31.12	25.16	150.8
1982	22.32	32.76	26.06	134.7
1983	22.21	32.90	26.01	126.1
1984	22.67	33.69	26.59	119.2

Source: Crandall *et al* (1986)

Table 7.10
Evidence of elasticities of traffic level to petrol price

	Explicit Short run	Long run	Ambiguous
Time series	-0.16 (0.08 to 4.00)	-0.33 (0.10 to 4.00)	-0.46 (0.40 to 5.00)
Cross section	....	-0.29 (0.06 to 2.00)	-0.5 (n.a. to 1)

Source: Goodwin (1992)

Some countries have also made explicit use of fixed charges as an element in their overall urban traffic congestion policy. Hong Kong, for example, trebled annual car tax in 1982 and doubled its purchase tax on cars with a consequential 20 percent reduction in car ownership. Valletta has higher car taxes than rural Malta - a specific disincentive to urban car ownership. Recently, the nature of some of these schemes has become quite innovative. In Singapore, for example, until May 1990 taxes (i.e. registration fees, import duties, etc.) made amounted to two-thirds of the purchase price of a car. The aim was to contain the growth in the national car park and equally, through such measures as area licensing and parking policies, to limit the use made of the park. Legislative reforms initiated in 1990 brought in a system of 10-year certification of ownership whereby a potential new car owner must enter a public tender to obtain the right to own a car. The difficulty is that the implementation of this quasi-market approach has tended to lead to speculation in licences (a problem encountered in many markets for durable products) which in turn questions the efficiency with which licences actually optimise traffic congestion.

Another innovation in Singapore has been the introduction of differential licences. If a new car is to be used only at weekends, when congestion is low, then there is preferential treatment in terms of lower fees, import duties, etc. The effect of these policies is less clear cut. The portfolio of transport measures employed in Singapore makes it difficult to isolate the effects of any specific instrument. In Hong Kong it appears that, certainly in the early 1980s, the high car taxes had much less impact on traffic in the congested parts of the colony than in the more rural areas, suggesting that they only partially met their objectives.

7.6   Subsidies

Subsidies can be treated in several entirely different ways. In one context there is the notion of the Pigouvian subsidy. This is simply the idea that by offering the appropriate subsidy to a perpetrator of a negative externality it is possible to bribe him to reduce his activities to the socially optimal level. It is often seen as the mirror image of the Pigouvian tax in that the same level of change can be brought about as with the tax but it is the tax payer who suffers the burden of payment rather than the polluter. Such payments are not unknown in transport and governments do give subsidies to transport suppliers to help cover the costs of reducing the environmental damage which they cause.

The Pigouvian subsidy, however, is somewhat more complex than it at first appears. Setting aside problems of cheating, a subsidy to reduce emissions has two effects. Assuming the subsidy takes the form of a payment (μ) for each unit of pollution (s) achieved by a vehicle below the optimal level (s*), then we can define a lump sum element and a tax element, i.e.:

total subsidy $= \mu(s^* - s) = \mu s^* - \mu s$

Any lump sum component (such as μs^*) does not affect how much pollution the vehicle emits but it does affect the number of vehicles because it shifts the average cost curve for car use - in this case it shifts it down. The result is that while each vehicle emits an optimal level of pollution, there will be too many vehicles leading to excessive pollution overall. The marginal subsidy could even lead to an increase in pollution. The problem can only be resolved with supplementary exit and entry controls.

Second there are subsidies to those affected by pollution and other environmental damage and which are given as compensation. Examples of this include compensation to households who live near noisy roads or airports or who suffer health damage as a result of pollution. Theoretically, however, if the number of victims is large this is an inappropriate economic strategy, although from a political perspective sometimes a difficult one to avoid. The relevant point can be made with reference to our noisy road example. If all people living adjacent to the road were fully compensated for the nuisance then there would be no incentive for anyone to move away to quieter locations. There would be an economic incentive to accept the ill effects of the noise with no offsetting benefits to anyone. Returning to the arguments of Chapter 5, there would also be no incentive to take optimal defensive actions (e.g. installing double-glazing) to reduce the impact of the environmental intrusion. This is essentially a moral hazard problem akin to the situation where the state insures individuals or firms against adverse outcomes; there is no incentive in such situations for risk-aversion strategies. One could, indeed, look upon compensation as a form of subsidised insurance.

More common in the transport field is the third broad type of subsidy. This is not given to the transport user causing environmental damage but rather to competitive services which are less environmentally intrusive or cause less congestion (e.g. Mohring, 1979). One of the common arguments for subsidising public transport, especially in urban areas, is that it causes less environmental damage than the private automobile. Of course, the situation is, in practice, somewhat more complex than this and the environmental justification is often heavily entwined with other motivating factors such as strict traffic management needs and equity arguments. However, the policy of subsidising both capital expenditures and operating costs of public transport modes for environmental reasons is well established in many Continental European countries and was an element in the UK's 1968 Transport Act.

The effects of subsidising an environmentally less harmful mode of transport can be seen by looking at the simple case illustrated in Figure 7.6. To avoid excessive complications we consider the alternative of subsidising a light rapid transit (LRT) as an alternative to the car. The LRT is assumed to have dedicated track so as to avoid problems of operation interactions and to be environmentally benign (that

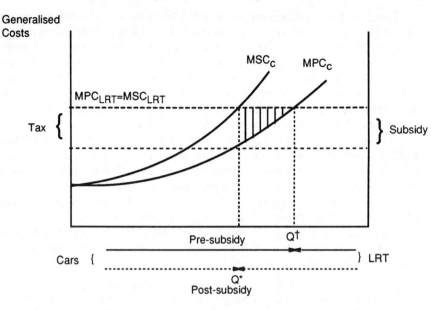

Figure 7.6
The impact of subsidising an environmentally benign transport mode

is, $MSC_{LRT}=MPC_{LRT}$). Fares are set at marginal cost which, again for ease of exposition, are assumed constant. In contrast, car use has significant adverse environmental externalities associated with it (i.e. $MSC_C>MPC_C$). We also assume that the total trips generated is fixed - which may not be too unrealistic in the short term for peak-hour journeys to work.

Since travellers base mode choice on observed private costs, the actual mode split which will emerge can be depicted as Q^t in the diagram - the mix of use at which, at the margin, travellers are indifferent, in marginal private cost terms, as to which mode is used. This is clearly not, however, the environmentally optimal mix. At the mode split Q^t, MSC_C exceeds the MSC_{LRT} and overall social benefits would be enhanced by travellers switching to the LRT system. Such a switch would occur if optimal environmental charges, internalising the negative externalities of car use, were introduced but in the absence of these the public mode may be subsidised to achieve the same diversionary effect.

The optimal level of subsidy is depicted in Figure 7.6. As can be seen it produces a mode split of Q^* which is identical to that with optimal environmental charges. One should note, however, that the subsidy strategy is very much a second-best option. There is a resource wastage associated with it (shown by the shaded area) which does not occur with the emission charge approach. This is because it is impossible to isolate each potential transferee from car to LRT and to tailor subsidies to the exact amount each individual would require in terms of reduced fees to bring about the necessary modal switch.

There are also some further problems with using subsidies. For a subsidy to be effective, it is important that there is a relatively high cross-elasticity between the modes involved. Without this a high subsidy, say, for public transport may prove totally ineffective in attracting users away from the private motor car. In addition, it is often important that no latent demand exists for road use which will simply result in current non-travellers on a network moving in to fill the space made available as existing users switch from car to public transport.

The traditional view was that the cross-elasticity between public transport and car use is not particularly high (Webster and Bly, 1980). In particular, there is limited scope for reversing trends although there may be some opportunity for slowing the take-up of car ownership by improving public transport services (Button *et al*, 1980). This has been supported by more recent analysis of direct fare elasticities by Goodwin (1992) who in surveying 50 studies found that the short-term elasticity seems to be about -0.41 which rises to about -0.55 after four years and to -0.65 after a decade. He concludes,

> Thus in the short term, bus demand remains, as traditionally thought, inelastic enough to make revenue raising by fare increases an effective policy, but demand increases by fare reductions (for example to assist congestion) rather limited. But in the longer run the effectiveness of the first policy is reduced, and of the second is increased.

This problem is compounded by two further points. First, is the issue of the degree to which there may be leakage from subsidies into, for example, X-inefficiency in the management of the system (e.g. see Pucher *et al*'s (1983) work on this topic). There are methods of tendering which, for example, are being used in the UK to minimise such losses but it is not altogether certain that they may not meet problems in the longer term as incumbent subsidised operators essentially enjoy economies of experience over potential new suppliers. Second, there is the question of the nature of the subsidy required. Fare subsidies, for example, may be of social importance in income distribution terms but often it is quality of service (i.e. frequency, reliability, amenities, etc.) which is of more importance to commuters.

Subsidies may, therefore, have a role to play in a second-best situation but their adoption, especially in the context of urban traffic issues, involves a rather more complex set of issues than is often taken into account. Subsidies have a political advantage, however, in that they involve transferring resources from a disparate population (either local or national tax payers, but more frequently a combination of the two) to a very visible and identifiable group of beneficiaries; in our case public transport users. Unlike direct pollution charges or less direct fiscal instruments, such as vehicle taxes or road pricing, which hit a specific group but which generate revenues which can be used to benefit society more generally, subsidies seldom adversely affect any particular interest group. Their financing, therefore, causes few complaints. This, to a large extent explains why, despite their numerous shortcomings, they are so widely used.

8   Non-fiscal Policy Instruments

8.1   Introduction

Fiscal instruments or the fuller allocation of property rights are generally favoured by economists when discussing environmental policy. In circumstances where there are high transactions costs or where for political reasons, such as concern over the distribution impacts of fiscal actions, other instruments may provide a more efficient means of attaining overall socially efficient outcomes. Indeed, much environmental policy has traditionally relied on non-fiscal tools and the political rationale for this is looked at in more detail in Chapter 9.

Here the main aim is to examine the nature of alternatives to fiscal measures. These options take a variety of different forms but often rely more on physical direction and controls to reduce the environmental intrusion caused by transport. In that sense, they fit into a very general framework of environmental management. The exact dividing line between fiscal and regulatory controls is not a simple one and the division is in some instances designed to provide continuity of argument rather than a perfect technical dichotomy. For example, we included tradeable permits in the previous chapter, but they might equally have been incorporated here as mechanisms for efficient attainment of a standard. Equally, investment, which is discussed below, might easily be viewed as a fiscal tool - it also, however, ties in with physical planning.

8.2   Regulations

Direct use of command-and-control instruments has in the past been the cornerstone of much environmental policy. At the most basic level, theoretically, if one can define the optimal environmental charge then one should be able to define the optimal level of environmental emissions - they are simply the two sides of the same coin. In Figure 8.1, for example, if one can define the pollution charge, P, to attain the optimal emissions reduction then sufficient information must exist to define the standard, R, which produces the identical result.

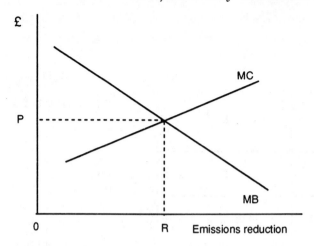

Figure 8.1
Regulations and charges

There may be a number of sound economic reasons for policy makers adopting a quantitative control rather than a fiscal one. (There may also be other reasons - see Chapter 9). It may simply be more costly in terms of administration, policing and monitoring to use fiscal instruments - this is, for example, an argument often used to favour limiting parking capacity rather than using road pricing to contain the adverse effects of urban traffic congestion. Related to this, in other instances, because of the nature of the problem, it may simply not be possible to devise a practical means of collecting charges.

Regulations take a wide variety of forms and often serve not only environmental objectives but also a diversity of other aims. The detailed forms of regulation are too numerous to set down, and even within broad groupings, varying considerably between countries or cities. A simple categorisation, though, following the lines of Table 7.1 may be helpful.

The command-and-control instruments may themselves take one of three broad forms. First, they may be imposed directly on the environmentally damaging agent itself. These can take the form, for instance, of:- vehicle noise limits (for instance, see Table 8.1); limits on the benzene and lead content of fuel (Table 8.2); controls over the cleaning of tankers' oil tanks; etc.

Perhaps more common than these direct measures are the two categories of indirect regulation. The first of these takes the form of controls over the use made of and the nature of vehicles used, for example, the fitting and wearing of seat belts; the fitting of catalytic converters; maximum vehicle sizes; physical traffic management measures (junction priorities, rights of way, etc.); double-hulling of ships; the number of engines required for commercial aircraft operating over water; etc.

Table 8.1

Vehicle noise emission limits in selected countries (D(b)), (ISO R362 - 1964)†

Country	Heavy Lorries			Small commercial		Buses		Cars	Motor-cycles
Weight (t)	>3.5			2.0-3.5	<2.0	Large	Small		
Power (kw)	>150	75-100	<75			>150	<150		
Australia									
Current	89	87	87	82	82	88	86	81	80
Future††	84	83	81	79	78	83	80	77	80
Japan	83		83	78		83	83	78	75
Switzerland	84	82	80	77		82	80	75	73-86
EC									
Current	88	86		81		85	82	80	82
Future	87*	83*	81*	78**	78**	83**	80**	77#	80##

† Tested by a microphone at height 1.2 metres & distance 7.5 metres from the centre line of vehicle

†† Standards consistent with C from 1992/3

* From 1st October 1990

** From 1st October 1988, diesel engines had until 1st October 1990

From 1st October 1988 for new type approvals

From 1995/6

Source: Organisation for Economic Cooperation and Development (1991)

Table 8.2
Gasoline lead content in selected OECD countries

Country	Maximum lead content of Leaded gasoline (g/l)
EC	0.013
Australia	0.013
Austria	0.013
Canada	0.290
Finland	0.150
Japan	0.004
Switzerland	0.000
United Kingdom	0.013
United States	0.026

The second group of indirect environmental regulations are those limiting the total amount of traffic: e.g. quantity licensing of taxicabs in cities (e.g. New York); pedestrianisation of city centres; parking permits, entry to city centres (e.g. Athens) on alternate days for odd and even number-plated cars,; banning of heavy lorry movements at weekends (e.g. France); and so on.

8.3 Charges versus Standards

Regulations of one sort or another are, therefore, widely used in the transport sphere but their appropriateness is not accepted by many. Economists in particular have regularly argued that, other than when there are excessively high transactions costs involved, fiscal policy in the form of emissions charges, road pricing, etc., is preferable on efficiency grounds to using emissions charges. The debate on the subject has been extensive and in many ways is inconclusive. Here we focus on just one or two of the arguments which have been advanced and seem of specific relevance to the transport sector. More general text on environmental economics, such as Baumol and Oates (1988) and Pearce and Turner (1990) and the recent survey of Cropper and Oates (1992) provide more thorough treatments.

One way of looking at the subject is to consider exactly what any form of regulation entails. If we take noise limits as an example then these involve stipulating a maximum level of noise allowed and imposing penalties, which are generally fines, on violators. In Figure 8.2 we suppose that, because of inadequate information concerning both the MEC and MNPB curves, the limit, S, is set too high and that in consequence it limits traffic to T^* rather than the optimum level of $T^\dagger$. In itself this is not a specific criticism of regulation; after all when confronted with imprecise information any noise tax could equally well be set at the wrong level. Suppose, however, that the penalty for violating the standard is set at P^*. This is also sub-optimal and, indeed, will encourage traffic to increase to level T'. This is simply because the

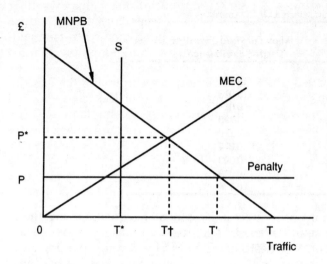

Figure 8.2
Potential problems with standards

penalty for violating the regulation is lower than the MNPB of continuing to travel until this traffic flow is reached.

One could argue that the penalty needs raising and the authorities should, given the number of violations, respond accordingly. In fact the situation is more complex than this in many cases because there may well be only a small probability of being caught and thus the penalty perceived by the road user (i.e. the fine multiplied by the chance of being caught) is lower than the level of fine in Figure 8.2. This does mean that regulations are always rather ineffectual. Much depends on ease of enforcement. In the noise case, if one were dealing with aircraft movements at an airport the environmental intrusion is relatively easy to monitor and fines to impose. It is a somewhat different picture regarding cars, lorries and motorcycles in a busy urban area.

Another line of argument involves the relative incentive effects of the two broad approaches for the take-up of new, cleaner technologies (e.g. Maler, 1974). The argument can be developed using Figure 8.3 which refers to car exhaust emissions. MC_1 is the marginal cost to the motorist of cleaning up exhaust emissions by applying retro, end-of-pipeline (not quite literally!) treatments to current exhaust technologies. MC_2 is the marginal cost of clean-up when a new technology has been adopted. We assume that an optimal pollution charge has been established to be P and a corresponding optimum standard for emissions would be C. The actual incentive effects relate to the relative costs of adopting the new technology under the different regimes. With charges, the motorist will reduce emissions to level C by paying CBD_1 for the end-of-pipeline treatment (this costing less than paying the charge for CD_1 emissions) and by paying OPBC for the OC emissions which he continues to emit (the benefit of doing this exceeding the emissions fees paid). To adopt the new technology would reduce these payments by ABD_1D_2. This is because the combined costs of end-of-pipeline treatment coupled with payment of emission charges amounts to only $OPAD_2$ with the new technology.

With the regulation, the cost of compliance employing the existing technology amounts to CBD_1 and there are no user fees to pay beyond this. Adopting the new technology reduces cost of compliance to CED_2 giving a financial incentive of D_2EBD_1 to do so. As can be seen, the differential incentive effect encouraging the adoption of the new, cleaner technology amounts to CED_2 (i.e. $D_2EBD_1 - ABD_1D_2$) in favour of the charging approach. In the longer term, therefore, it would appear that fiscal measures provide a greater stimulus to the up-take of less environmentally damaging innovations than do charges.

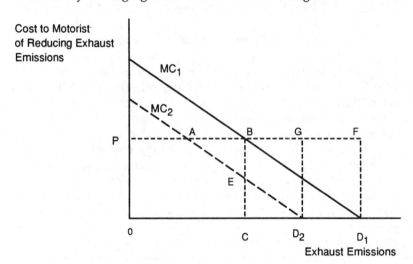

Figure 8.3
The incentives case for charges over regulation

There are some caveats, however, which need to be mentioned. The analysis does make rather strong assumptions regarding motorists' perceptions. In particular, it assumes perfect myopia regarding the level of charges or the nature of the standard. In other words P and S are assumed invariant with respect to the actions of motorists. What would happen in practice is that as the new technology is taken up so the optimum pollution charge or emissions standard should be adjusted - essentially the shift in the MEC curve produces a new equilibrium point. It is quite easy to see that if motorists were aware of this then their incentive to adopt the new technology would be the same for both a fiscal or regulatory regime. How myopic people are is unclear. The Maler model may be relatively realistic for the large group situation - few motorists would anticipate that their individual actions would influence pollution charge levels or legal standards - but may be less realistic when dealing with sectors such as aviation or railways where there are many fewer actors involved.

Most arguments surrounding the charging versus standards debate have assumed that policy makers have good information regarding the MNPB and MEC curves. In a seminal paper, Weitzman (1974) showed that if there is asymmetric information then, depending on the relative steepness of the curves, one type of policy is preferable to the other. If the MNPB curve is steep but the MEC curve relatively shallow (e.g. there may be some form of threshold effect below which the pollutant is harmless but beyond which its impact is severe) then there is a need for close control over emissions levels. If a price instrument were used and the price under-estimated because the true costs of pollution had not been realised then the critical level of pollution could be exceeded. Weitzman advocates a standard be set in such circumstances.

Alternatively, if the MEC curve has a steeper absolute slope than the MNPB curve, then the setting of an overly stringent standard would impose excessive costs on the polluter and society more generally. A price regime under these conditions will give some flexibility allowing polluters to pay a high emissions charge but at least their activities would not entirely be curtailed. Of course, theoretically, the way around this type of problem more generally is to employ a combination of the tools with a standard being established with the possibility of additional units of 'pollution' being purchased beyond that and subsidies to produce below it. How this might operate in most transport markets is difficult to envisage although it might be possible where there are a small number of polluters (e.g. ships in ports or airlines at airports).

A final argument, not unrelated to the last, which has been advanced in favour of charging concerns its advantages when there is incomplete information about either the aggregate MNPB or MEC curves or the specific ones confronting individual polluters (Baumol and Oates, 1988). In these circumstances neither the optimal charge nor standard can be defined with any precision. Given these conditions, it is the emissions charge which provides a more efficient method of attaining any desired level reduced pollution. It is, in a sense, more cost-effective than the emissions standard. By way of illustration, in Figure 8.4 we plot out the marginal abatement costs for NO_X emissions in two cities, A and B. The curves are not known with any degree of exactitude to policy makers. Since with no intervention there will be excessive pollution it is decided, on the basis of what is known, that a 20 percent reduction in NO_X emissions would be generally beneficial. A mandatory reduction of 20 percent in each city would result in emissions being reduced to A and B respectively in the two cities. While the desired objective has been satisfied, what one sees is that the MAC costs involved differ as between the cities - they are higher in city A than B. It would be more cost effective to reduce NO$_X$ levels by a larger amount in B than A quite simply because it is cheaper per unit to cut emissions in the former. A pollution charge of P per unit of emissions would automatically achieve the aimed for improvement because it would be more of an incentive to cut pollution where it is cheaper to do so (i.e. a level B† in city B) and have smaller reductions where the costs of abatement are higher (i.e. to A†)

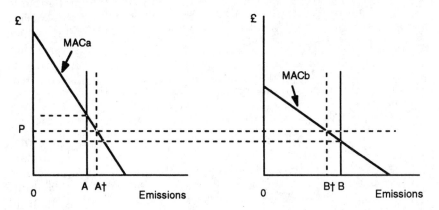

Figure 8.4
The advantage of fiscal instruments when there is uncertainty

Of itself the Baumol and Oates argument is not one that establishes fiscal tools as superior to regulations. Rather it highlights the fact that if a particular standard is to be aimed for then the most efficient way of attaining it is by using fiscal instruments. One can see the particular importance of this in many transport contexts. Because of its very nature much transport activity is a mobile source of environmental intrusion but the domains in which it operates often differ in their sensitivity to its presence. Different airports, for example, because of their location and prevailing wind conditions impose different noise envelopes on their surrounding populations. The actual physical noise associated with any aircraft type may, therefore, impose different costs at different airports. To set a standard that all aircraft should reduce noise levels by a specified amount would thus be inefficient. A charge, on the other hand which would bring about the same overall noise reduction would give the flexibility to airlines to use their quieter aircraft at locations where noise is a major nuisance and their older, noisier ones where the problem is less severe.

In some circumstances, however, there may be political advantages in using marketable permits as opposed to emissions charging to attain the desired standard. The point is clearly made by Cropper and Oates (1992):

A major advantage of the marketable permit approach is that it gives the environmental authority direct control over the quantity of emissions. Under the fee approach, the regulator must set a fee, and if, for example, the fee turns out to be too low, pollution will exceed permissible levels. The agency will find itself in the uncomfortable position of having to adjust and readjust the fee to ensure that the environmental standard is attained. Direct control over quantity is to be preferred since the standard itself is prescribed in quantity terms.

As we see in the next chapter, however, while all these types of argument over the welfare pros and cons of fiscal measures versus command-and-control policies may attract considerable attention amongst academic economists the decision over which strategy to adopt tends to be decided on other, wider criteria.

8.4   Land-Use and Transport Planning

Land-use planning has a long history. While such planning is usually designed to meet a diverse range of objectives, and employs an extensive portfolio of instruments in order to try and attain them, protection and the enhancement of the environment is now often a high priority. While land-use planning is not entirely an urban activity, much of relevance to transport intrusion is done at the urban level.

In transport terms, a key document in this context is the Buchanan Report, *Traffic in Towns* (UK Ministry of Transport, 1963). This concluded,

> There are absolute limits to the amount of traffic that can be accepted in towns, depending upon their size and density, but up to these limits, provided a civilised environment is to be retained or created, the level of vehicular accessibility a town can have depends on its readiness to accept and pay for the physical changes required. The choice is society's.

The underlying thesis of the report, was that the automobile was likely to continue as the dominant mode of transport and that carefully designed road space should be provided to accommodate forecast increases in traffic with the caveat that such accessibility would have to be limited to preserve environmentally acceptable areas for pedestrians, which combined safety, quietness and a minimum of atmospheric pollution. A number of case studies were presented to show how this could be achieved.

While the Buchanan philosophy was influential in transport - land use planning, the resources required to carry out the necessary reconstruction of urban areas simply were not available to carry it through in its fullness. Additionally, the planning methodology embraced little by way of policy recommendations for coping with traffic which exceeded the limits which were deemed tolerable in urban areas. In other words the planning offered blueprints for cities which could accommodate a level of traffic without serious local environmental degradation but it offered little by way of advice on how to manage the traffic.

A more recent efforts at redesigning land-use to minimise car travel is the Dutch strategy of locating new commercial developments around major public transport interchanges (*ABC lokatiebeleid*) - see van Huut (1991). Also, although less directly of immediate relevance to the congestion issue, we find in the former East Germany that, confronted with transport constraints, industrial development policy is aimed at geographically concentrating economic activities rather than spreading them. At a more micro-level, the development of traffic cells as an integral part of the land-use architecture in some western cities (Organisation for Economic Cooperation and Development, 1988c) and of auto-restraint zones in the US (Herald, 1977) can be seen as elements of this land-use planning approach.

Since land-use planning is a long-term exercise the ultimate implications for these land-use/transportation strategies will not materialise for some time. However, retrospectively, efforts to engineer travel behaviour through land-use planning (for example, in the UK context this would embrace such things as new towns and overspill policy) have not been conspicuously successful. There is evidence that traffic cells and pedestrianisation have produced some beneficial regeneration effects in central urban areas which, in turn, act to limit the spread of congestion to suburban sites. At the same time, however, this can lead to additional traffic in the immediate surrounding areas. By-pass facilities are often seen as key components of land-use/transportation planning which, by causing through-traffic to avoid congested core areas, reduce demand for congested road space (UK Department of Transport, 1989c). In itself, however, the policy may prove of limited effectiveness without accompanying sticks to divert traffic to what is often a physically longer route. In practice, the traffic effects of by-pass and circular road construction are difficult to forecast as witnessed by the case of the M25 Motorway around London which attracted considerable, and unexpected, local traffic.

8.5   Investments

The notion that one should, given the imperfections of markets, incorporate non-financial implications of transport investments when deciding on the actions to pursue is not new and in many ways has its origins in Adam Smith's discussions of canals. What has happened over the past thirty years is that the theory of exactly how this might be done has been refined and the practical tools with which to actually do it have been developed. In particular, economists and transport engineers have expended considerable energies in the field of cost-benefit analysis.

While dated, perhaps the best description of exactly what such analysis involves is provided by Prest and Turvey (1965), namely:

> CBA is a practical way of assessing the desirability of projects, where it is important to take a long view (in the sense of looking at repercussions in the further as well as the nearer future) and a wide view (in the sense of allowing for the side effects of many kinds on many persons, industries, regions, etc.) - i.e. it implies the enumeration and evaluation of all the relevant costs and benefits.

Taken quite literally, one can interpret this in terms of the following mathematical formulation;

$$NPV = \sum_{n=1}^{k} \sum_{m=1}^{j} \left\{ \frac{P(a_m B_{mn}) - P(b_m C_{mn})}{(1+r)^n} \right\}$$

where:-

NPV   is the social net present value;

$P(a_m B_{mn})$ is the probable social benefit to be enjoyed by individual m in year n as a result of the investment's completion. B_{mn} is given a weighting a_m to reflect society's welfare preference;

$P(b_m C_{mn})$ is the probable social cost to be enjoyed by individual m in year n as a result of the investment's completion. C_{mn} is given a weighting b_m to reflect society's welfare preference;

$(1+r)^n$ is the relative social weight attached to a cost or benefit occurring in a given year;

k   is the anticipated life of the investment;

j   is the total number of individuals affected.

   While substantial, the equation is not difficult to follow. The problem is that full implementation has yet to be achieved despite considerable resources being expended on large-scale CBA exercises such as the UK's study for the siting of a third London airport in the 1970s (Commission on the Third London Airport, 1971) and the widespread use of quasi-CBA techniques, such as the COBA package for trunk roadappraisal used by the UK Department of Transport (1989a), as regular components of project assessment. Equally, in some other countries (see Table 8.3) such as Sweden a wide range of factors are built into transport investment appraisal which brings it close to the theoretical model in the context of coverage although not in terms of the use of common monetary units of valuation. In many countries, however, the appraisal process is much less developed (see Table 8.4) and poorly integrated into the wider, strategic, transport-planning process.

   Many of the difficulties are not strictly to do with the incorporation of environmental factors into this framework - they stem from such theoretical problems as the legitimacy of applying a partial equilibrium approach to large schemes with potentially general equilibrium implications and from such practical problems as deciding upon the appropriate weighting schemes when assessing distribution consequences across affected groups - but certainly questions of how to include a complete environmental assessment in a way consistent with the monetary evaluation of other factors has consistently arisen. The difficulties which can arise, for example, if this is not done are illustrated by the methods of road investment appraisal used in the UK.

Table 8.3
Major components of the Swedish project analysis model for road investment

Traffic economy and road maintenance	Environmental and land-use effects	Regional development etc.
Traffic safety*[†]	Noise*[†]	Regional balance
Travel time*	Air pollution[†]	Effects for trade,
Comfort[†]	Barrier effects[†]	industry and tourism
Vehicle costs*	Water supply	
Maintenance*	Vibrations	
	Landscape/scenery	
	Nature conservation	
	Land development*	

* Effects evaluated in monetary terms based on willingness to pay
[†] Effects evaluated in monetary terms based on explicit public preferences

At the strategic level, a roads programme is developed for the country setting out the broad network for future investment. The strategy is based mainly upon perceived economic needs of the country, regional equity and similar criteria. At the next level, detailed analysis of potential traffic and other effects is carried out to decide upon alignment, design standards, etc. The UK Department of Transport has for many years employed the COBA computer package in this latter stage to evaluate road investment in terms of user impacts (embracing travel time, vehicle operating cost and accident impacts expressed in monetary terms and discounted over an extended time horizon). Following the advice of the Leitch Committee (UK Department of Transport, 1978), the Department has treated environmental and other non-user aspects separately in a project impact matrix. The latter is a matrix of local effects expressed in physical or verbal terms and set against the various parties affected. A *Manual of Environmental Appraisal* sets out methods of analysis to ensure that a level of consistency is achieved across studies. While such an approach has the advantage that at least third-party effects are considered, in practice the coverage of the matrix tends to be limited to local environmental impacts (noise, lead, visual intrusion, etc.) and inter-temporal effects are seldom included.

More seriously, the overall decision process has an observed tendency to give greater emphasis to what appears to be the more scientific and condensed evidence contained in the COBA output than to the less transparent information set out in the impact matrix. Indeed, the UK House of Commons Select Committee on Public Accounts (1989) has come to this very conclusion and pressed for a more systematic treatment of the diverse implications of transport investment. Specifically it stated,

> We regard the evaluation of the environmental effects as important in arriving at sound decisions on the roads programme, and we recommend that the

Table 8.4

States of transport infrastructure decision-making procedures in selected European countries

	France	Germany	Italy	Belgium	Sweden	Denmark	Norway	Finland	Switz.
Systems approach	S	M	S	S	M	M	M	S	W
Master plan	M	W	M	S	M	M	M	S	W
Intermodal cooperation	S	M	S	S	S	M	S	S	M
Time horizon	Long	Long	Short	Short	Medium	Short	Medium	Medium	Long
Private financing	M	S	S	S	S	S	S	S	S

S = Scarcely developed
M = Partially developed
W = Well developed

Source: Roundtable of European Industrialists (1987)

Department should address this issue more determinedly, supported as necessary by further research...

The outcome has been a set of recommendations from the Stand-
ing Advisory Committee on Trunk Road Assessment (UK Department
of Transport, 1992) that have partially been adopted by government. In
particular it was argued that there is the need for consistency in the
treatment of environmental impacts throughout any appraisal exercise and that such impacts should not simply be considered in impact
matrix form at the final stage, *viz.*:

> In order to ensure that proper account is taken of all effects, the appropri-
> ate environmental assessments must underlie every stage in the decisions, from
> the making of national and regional policy downwards. Different effects can-
> not be neatly compartmentalised or allocated exclusively to one particular
> point in that hierarchy.

With regard to the specific issue of whether monetary valuations
should be more widely used, the Committee recognised that 'There are
some environmental effects which cannot sensibly be valued....' but
equally argued that there is no reason why those, such as noise, where
there is a well-established body of evidence, should not be.

These types of modification to the cost-benefit approach are likely
to lead to a more consistent treatment of environmental effects but
there is a more fundamental point about infrastructure provision. It
has been argued (Wheaton, 1978) that the conventional cost-benefit
analysis approach to appraisal, because of its inherent assumptions regarding pricing, can lead to over-investment in transport infrastructure and excessive transport use. In Figure 8.5 we show various combinations of prices charged for road use and, on the vertical, various

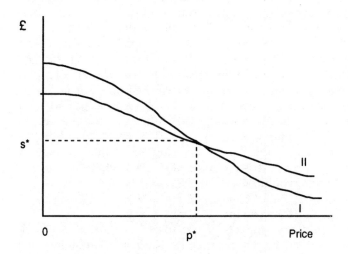

Figure 8.5
Second-best investment with sub-optimal congestion pricing

levels (in money terms) of investment. There will be some optimal price-investment mix such as P*/S* which is optimal. This would be the socially efficient outcome if road users were charged optimal prices (embracing all external considerations) for their journeys.

Suppose, however, that the price in effect does not fully reflect costs then, since there would be a heavy demand for road use, the conventional cost-benefit analysis approach would imply that more investment than S* is required. Curve I traces out the relevant optimal price-investment combinations which would emerge. In fact, the low price is generating demand beyond the optimal level and thus the overall amount of traffic on curve I at points to the left will be sub-optimally large. Wheaton argues, therefore, that investment should be limited along a P/S curve such as II. The additional congestion occurring at any price below P* because of the limited additional investment in capacity will in effect constrain traffic flows to the optimal level. The reasoning behind this conclusion is summarised by Wheaton in the following way:

> Such a reduction will increase congestion, and this helps to discourage the demand which has been 'artificially' induced by under pricing. It is important to remember that second-best investment does not call for building fewer road as the price of driving is lowered. That would result in 'excessive' congestion. Rather it requires accommodating less of the induced demand than would be met if a simple cost-benefit analysis were applied.

Applying this to the question of environmental policy, the relevance is mainly in terms of just how much investment in new infrastructure is economically justified when transport prices do not reflect true costs. The standard methodology tends to ignore the imperfections which exist in terms of transport users not paying for the full costs of their activities and thus to favour high levels of investment. Wheaton's analysis essentially implies that in these conditions where money prices are ineffective, second-best criteria determined by travellers time costs (i.e. congestion) can be used to limit travel to a level closer to the optimum. The actual conditions for achieving this second-best situation may, however, prove to be rather complex (Friedlaender, 1981). In terms of equity there may be a further argument in favour of such an approach in that time is allocated even across individuals. Practically, there are difficulties in working out the optimal second-best strategy and, in overall environmental terms, given the proportionately higher pollution, noise and other costs associated with congested roads it is not altogether clear what the ultimate overall social outcome would be.

8.6   Physical Traffic Management

Local urban environmental impacts of transport have often been tackled by means of physical traffic management strategies involving such things as one-way traffic flows, traffic signal timings, speed limits, junction priorities, bus lanes, etc. These often involve investment in particular equipment to facilitate the management but can usefully be distinguished from investment simply to provide additional physical capacity to the system. The aims of traffic management are diverse and embrace efforts at speeding traffic through the road network, giving priority to social service operations and handling different intensities of demand across the system as well as being seen as an environmental policy instrument.

In terms of environmental impacts, these differ according to the details of the schemes employed and the priorities set. In general the environment, with the exception of safety considerations, is given a somewhat lower priority than is the improvement of traffic-flow conditions. Indeed, in many cases to achieve a faster flow traffic is encouraged to take longer, but more rapid routings which can have mixed impacts on the environment. Generally it involves directing through-traffic in particular to more circumferential routes which impose less local environmental intrusion but it can lead to greater fuel use with the implications of this for the wider environment. Two recent developments in physical traffic management are, however, worth particular attention.

The first of these involves developments in telematics. A considerable amount of traffic congestion in cities is caused not by the sheer volume of cars, lorries and buses seeking to use roads but by poor information about optimal routing. Some of this is due to ignorance of where congestion is occurring and hence the inability to avoid adding to it but often accidents, breakdowns and other 'incidents' create bottlenecks in the network which are impossible to predict. Improved telematics and information systems can reduce many of these problems. On-vehicle information and route guidance systems are rapidly being developed and some basic systems are now used in countries like Japan. They can also reduce the amount of certain types of traffic - for example, improved electronic data interchange (EDI) systems, by increasing load factors and enhancing the productivity of vehicles, can reduce the empty running of goods vehicles. In a way this is the information management equivalent of efficient traffic management and like it, it will help improve the internal efficiency of the road network and can assist in reducing local traffic nuisance.

Second, there is traffic calming. This entails the use of such things as road humps, speed tables, raised junctions, reduced carriageway widths and 'changed road surfaces' to both slow traffic flows and to encourage the use of particular 'suitable' links in the network or alternative modes. Essentially the idea is to make streets more attractive and liveable. In Europe traffic calming has tended to come about as part of wider packages and has often been tied to legal speed limits of 30kph and, in the Netherlands, to a walking pace limit. The latter is part of the country's *Woonerven* - where road users have equal rights to road space. In the UK, traffic calming schemes have come about more as part of a policy to reduce urban traffic speed for safety reasons - about

70 percent of schemes have this as a primary objective. Evidence from Germany suggests that serious casualties have fallen by up to 50 percent in areas where it has been introduced, for example by 44 percent in Heidelberg.

8.7   Alternatives to Transport

Transport provides particular types of services but, as we have emphasised throughout, at a considerable environmental cost. One policy approach to containing and possibly reducing this cost is to encourage the use of alternatives to transport which offer similar services but with significantly lesser detrimental effects for the environment (Button, 1991b). Transferring both individual contacts and also document exchanges from physical to electronic movements is one way which has been advocated. Essentially telecommunications could be substituted for transport. Of course, the environmental advantages of the greater use of telecommunications are not quite as simple as they might appear at first sight.

Telecommunications have gone through something of a revolution over the past thirty years and the implications of the resultant changes are slowly beginning to be felt in a wider sphere. There is undoubtedly a link between transport and communications but this link is not always clear. In some instances telecommunications have been seen to represent a substitute for transport while in others they complement it.

There was a clear feeling a decade or so ago that in the post-industrial society manufacturing and service industries would be replaced by information industries. Indeed, to a considerable extent this has happened. According to one estimate, even in 1967 over 53 percent of total employee compensation in the US was tied to the generation, processing, transmission and management of information (Poret, 1976). Linked with this vision, however, was a perception that the advances in communications which have accompanied this process would exercise an important impact over travel behaviour by individuals and the transport used by industry (Nilles *et al*, 1976).

Despite this, subsequent work on the links between telecommunications and transport has tended to be spasmodic and often lacking in co-ordination (Salomon, 1985; 1988). The explanation for this is difficult to find especially given the potential benefits which the substitution of telecommunications for transport could potentially bring in terms of reduced congestion, energy savings, reduced pollution (both local, in terms of noise, vibration, etc., and global, in terms of lower emissions of global warming gases) and lower accident rates (Salomon, 1984).

Developments in telecommunications may be seen to have the potential for exerting both direct and indirect effects on transport. The direct effects stem from the short-term impact on transport use itself. This may embrace trip generation, mode choice, trip distribution and

assignment. Further, it may influence the temporal pattern of transport use e.g. leading to spreading of the peak. The indirect effects stem
from the longer-term implications of developments in telecommunications which may influence choices concerning residential, commercial and industrial location (see Nijkamp and Salomon, 1989). Ultimately this should, in turn, influence the transport infrastructure
provisions which are made and the ways in which they are used.

The literature looking at the links between transport and telecommunications is an expanding one nevertheless, as Salomon (1985) says,
'... there is scant empirical evidence on the relationship between travel
and telecommunications' - a view which echoes that of Tyler (1979)
made some years earlier which pointed to, '... the dearth of basic research on the interaction between telecommunications and the remainder of the economy'.

The field of telecommunications is advancing rapidly and with it
has developed a fairly extensive and specialised vocabulary.

• *Teleworking* embraces 'all work-related substitutions of telecommunications and related information technologies for travel (from
substitution of telephone calls or electronic mail for personal visits to
the use of full-information video conferencing as a substitute for exec-
utive travel)' (Nilles, 1988). Within this we have:-
  - *telecommuting*, which is the substitution of telecommunications for the commute to work. Telecommuting can itself be divided between home-based telecommuting, whereby the individual works from the home base, and regional-centre
  telecommuting.
  - *teleconferencing*, which permits the linking up of individuals while at work and may be seen in some cases as a substitute
  for actual work travel. The development of telefax, electronic
  mail, telex, etc. performs a similar function with regard to the
  transfer of paper documentation and videotex systems for business information more generally. These developments may influence the amount and nature of travel undertaken as part of
  work. One should also perhaps include in this categorisation
  the various forms of distance learning which are available and
  may influence the amount of school and college travel.
• *Telecommunications* may be seen as both a substitute for recre-
ational-based travel (e.g. the television or video at home rather than a
trip to the cinema) and household activity travel. In the latter context
we have:
  - *teleshopping*, which is the presentation in the home of information about available products; the ability to order them
  and have them delivered, has been viewed by some as a possible
  substitute for shopping trips. -
  - *home and office banking systems*, which may be seen as
  particular cases of teleshopping. In addition to this, the wider
  use of telecommunications within traditional shopping frame-

works may also influence travel behaviour. The development
of various forms of 'smart cards' now offers more flexibility in
the context of such things as using facilities located at banks but
out of traditional banking hours.

The important issue from the point of view of substitutability is
deciding what are the particular characteristics of journeys where
transfers to telecommunications are likely in any significant number.
Time constraints exert an important influence over communication
media choice and the need for timely decision making and
communication in today's business environment is increasing. Time
constraints can be measured both in terms of how long in advance a
meeting needs to be planned, and the total time taken up in getting to,
contacting, and returning from the meeting. Electronic media have
advantages over travel alternatives on both these criteria. As a
consequence, given time constraints, even if face-to-face contact is
preferred, telecommunications may become increasingly important.

In this context, some authors talk of a telecommunications gap, i.e.,

> The 'telecommunications gap' reflects ..... the increase in the use of telecommu-
> nication services caused by physical constraints of persons who have a poten-
> tially exponential growth curve for human interaction' (Nijkamp and Sa-
> lomon, 1989).

In developing this argument, Nijkamp and Salomon point to the
current organisation of socio-economic life in Western economies
which is based upon increasing levels of interpersonal contact (i.e.
face-to-face contact). There are, however, constraints on the physical
ability of individuals to engage in increasing numbers of interactions
in this way and, given a fixed time constraint, ultimately there must be
a limit (saturation level) beyond which additional personal contacts
just cease to be possible - see Figure 8.6. In consequence, while in the
short term there may be enhancement effects and synergy between
telecommunications and transportation this cannot endure.

If there are to be ultimate substitutions then these are unlikely to
relate to all forms of transport or trip. Maggi (1989) is primarily concerned with developing an analytical framework which can be used to
develop a cost model of communicating which offers a theoretical basis for deciding which types of trips are more amenable to substitution.
He develops a theoretical framework suggesting that distance may be
one of the main determining factors influencing degrees of substitution.

The main difference in communicating information by face-to-face
contact and telecommunications is in terms of time costs. Face to face
communications provide the maximum available transmission capacity (e.g. involving immediate interactions, visual gestures, use of visual aids, etc.) whereas with telecommunications the time costs of
sending complex messages rise rapidly and may become prohibitive.

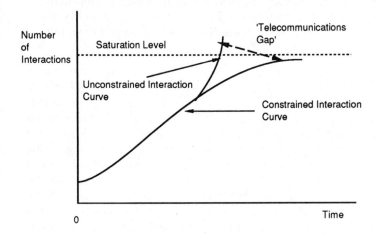

Figure 8.6
The telecommunications gap

The relevance of distance in this context can be seen by considering Figure 8.7. This shows the total costs of making contacts by face-to-face contact which involve transport or through the use of telecommunications. There are assumed to be negligible fixed costs associated with face-toface contacts but in the case of telecommunications there is assumed to be a need for investment in human capital (e.g. learning how to use electronic mail). In case (A) we have the combination short distance/low complexity of message. Here the costs of information transfer are low for both face-to-face contacts and telecommunications and hence the former will dominate unless contacts are very frequent per period of time. In (B) the combination is of short distance/high complexity of message. The high marginal cost involved in using telecommunications here suggests an almost total dominance of face-to-face contacts even where contacts are very frequent. Substitution is, therefore, unlikely.

Case (C) representing the combination of long distance/low complexity of message is an instance where there is a probability of substitution when a substantial number of contacts are made - essentially it is then worth investing in the human capital required to use the telecommunications media. Finally, in case (D) - long distance/high complexity of message - there is little likelihood of substitution because of the relative marginal costs involved. This is, however, an area where rapid technical progress is taking place (for example, in terms of developing video conferencing, videotext, telefax, videophones, etc.). Consequently, if the marginal costs of telecommunications are reduced, albeit possibly at the expense of a higher fixed cost, then these new forms of telecommunication may substitute for transport where contacts are frequent.

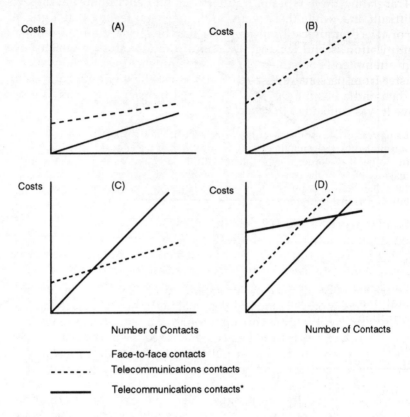

Figure 8.7
The fixed and variable cost trade-offs in telecommunications

Empirical work seeking to assess the environmental implications of encouraging the use of telecommunications in place of personal movements is limited and the findings rather inconclusive. Much of the work that has been done has been concerned with the level of potential transfers (see the material surveyed in Button, 1991b and Salomon, 1985). The European Conference of Ministers of Transport (1983), for example, estimated that the potential substitution for business trips was between 13 percent and 23 percent, for shopping trips of between 10 percent and 30 percent and for commuting trips of between 13 percent and 24 percent. Nilles (1988) and Garrison and Deakin (1988) suggest a potential substitution of around 10 percent for commuting trips in the US, while in the Netherlands it has been forecast that over the next 35 years there is unlikely to be more than an 8 percent switch to telecommuting although this will have a disproportionate effect on traffic by reducing peaks in congestion (Netherlands Organisation for Applied Scientific Research, 1989).

Translating these types of traffic effects into environmental impacts is difficult and, while there seems to be a general feeling that a greater use of telecommunications would be beneficial for the environment, quantification is still lacking. In one of the few studies which have been attempted, Boghani *et al* (1991) attempted to assess how such a transfer from personal transport would affect the environment. Using US data and adjusting the ECMT potential transfer parameters set out above it was concluded that,

> Using reasonable estimates for the percentage of the transportation activities substituted by telecommunications, we determined the annual societal benefits to be of the order of $23 billion, with the urban areas getting the vast majority (93%) of the benefits. In terms of other units, we estimate savings of 1.8 million tons of regulated pollutants, 3.5 billion gallons of gasoline, and 3.1 billion personal hours.

Similar work in the UK relating solely to videoconferencing and based upon a number of scenarios concerning future price changes in videoconferencing (up to 70 percent), introduction of standardisation of equipment, provision of infrastructure, future unrestrained traffic demand, etc., and making use of Quinet's (1990) values for environmental damage, generated the predictions for potential benefits from substitution for business travel seen in Table 8.5.

Table 8.5
The potential environmental benefits of videoconferencing in the UK (in 1989 prices)

Impact	2000 Alternative assumptions		2010 Alternative assumptions	
	Low	High	Low	High
Congestion:				
road	£417.67m	£930.04m	£664.44m	£1440.21m
air	Some	Some	Some	Some
Energy	Substantial +	Substantial +	Substantial +	Substantial +
Accidents	£136.83m	£273.66m	£177.06m	£312.69m
Pollution	£24.56m	£54.84m	£39.08m	£84.72m
Noise	£6.14 m	£13.71m	£9.77m	£21.18m
Land take	Negligible +	Negligible +	Negligible +	Negligible +
Aesthetics	Negligible -	Negligible -	Negligible -	Negligible -
Total*	£585.20m	£1272.25m	£890.35m	£1858.80m
Counterfactual	£117.04m	£190.25m	£ 273.96	£484.90m

* Only includes those items where monetary evaluation has been attempted
Source: Button and Lauder (1991)

8.8   Transhipment and Consolidation

So far most of our discussion has focused on passenger transport but the movement of goods also has important environmental implications and has been the subject of non-fiscal regulation. Freight transport is increasingly carried by road. This is in part due to the change in product mix involved (i.e. more manufacturers and less bulk raw materials), but also results from the wider use of just-in-time (JIT) management (Schneider, 1985). This essentially involves producers minimising inventories of finished goods and inputs by operating transport as an integrated part of the production process. To ensure both a steady inflow of components and of raw materials combined with rapid dispatch of final output to customers requires reliable and fast transport. Simple financial cost minimisation, therefore, gives way to trade-offs of cost against speed and reliability. The adoption of JIT techniques does not just affect the way production is carried on but often requires new manufacturing hardware and this has long term implications for such things as industrial location patterns. As Drucker (1990) says, with JIT,

> ...the plant no longer functions as a step-by-step process that begins at the receiving dock and ends when finished goods move into the shipping room. Instead, the plant must be redesigned from the end backwards as an integrated flow.

Exactly how widely JIT techniques are used is difficult to say. Certainly asking producers seems to shed little light on the question with many claiming to have fully integrated JIT systems but holding demonstrably high inventories while others, claiming little if any knowledge of the textbook JIT model, appear to have intuitively adopted it. Scanning the literature suggests that in the UK, which is certainly not the most innovative European country in this area, about 10 to 15 percent of firms employ effective JIT systems but this compares with over 40 percent in the US and 70 percent in Japan.

This greater use of more direct transportation services obviously has environmental implications. Essentially it means substitution of transport for other inputs into the production process. Since pollution and other environmental costs of this transport are not transparent to users there is a *prima facie* case for suspecting that its use will be suboptimal. The reduced holding of inventories (which saves financial costs) is achieved to a considerable extent by reducing consolidation and transhipment of goods at places such as warehouses and bulk breaking depots (which imposes environmental costs). In particular, the incentive to seek full loads and to minimise empty running time is reduced if the social costs of this are not borne by the user. Figure 8.8 provides the reasoning behind this.

The average load is used as a proxy for the amount of consolidation which is taking place. This can be justified since transhipment and consolidation reduces empty running by matching consignments

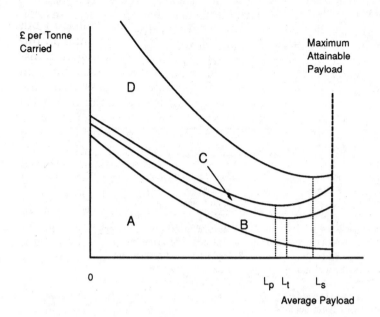

Figure 8.8
The distribution of costs associated with levels of transhipment

more closely to final customers. The transport industry's direct concern in the absence of mechanisms to internalise environmental costs is to minimise its combined haulage (A) and consolidation (B) costs. Since the cost per tonne carried will fall with greater utilisation, the haulage cost curve slopes down in relation to average payload. Consolidation costs tend to fall with average payload initially, as the overheads associated with depots can be spread more widely, but then rise as the complexity of matching loads to vehicles becomes more difficult. The minimum combined cost A + B suggests that the transport sector would seek an average pay-load of L_t in the diagram. However, the sector must also take account of the demands confronting it. Customers, especially those engaged in JIT practices, seek speedy delivery with delays being seen as particularly expensive. Collecting and resorting at consolidation depots increase the time to delivery/collection (C). If this element is added to the transport sectors costs then the optimal amount of consolidation (average payload), which will be the one achieved in practice, falls to L_p. The more JIT management is adopted so L_p will move to the left and the average payload will decline.

Introducing environmental costs (D) into the diagram shows that L_p is sub-optimally low. The environmental costs of consolidation tend to fall as the average payload increases. This is because some of the environmental costs are fixed (e.g. unsightly depots) while many others are related to the number of vehicle movements which varies inversely with average payload. Additionally, there are thresholds which once exceeded make it viable to use specialised, less environmentally intrusive vehicles for such things as urban delivery/collection. Once these costs are incorporated the optimal level of consolidation is at an average payload of L_s, considerably higher than when the environmental dimension is ignored.

Table 8.6
The costs and benefits of transhipment

Costs	Benefits
1. Capital costs of depot	1. Economies of scale in trunk
2. Operating costs of depot	haulage
3. Administrative costs	2. Environmental benefits from
4. Damage to the environment	smaller vehicles in urban areas
surrounding the depot	3. Regular collections/deliveries
5. Reduced frequency of collection	4. Reduced lorry movements
delivery in city centres	5. Reductions in fleet size and
6. Provision of additional storage	haulage manpower
space and the need to hold	6. Fuel savings
large stocks of goods within city	
7. Efficiency losses due either to	
the use of specialised vehicles	
or general purpose vehicles	
8. Generated motor-car traffic	
9. Damage and theft	

Note: In individual cases some of these items may take negative values and effectively switch columns.
Source: Button and Pearman (1981)

The incorporation of environmental costs into the users, decision processes via measures such as pollution charges would, of course, automatically lead to a payload of L_p. If this is not done then legal requirements to consolidate more consignments, especially on the outskirts of cities, have been advocated. Regulations could be framed which would lead to a socially optimal average payload but in practice it would prove difficult to define levels of consolidation for each type of commodity carried and for each type of vehicle used. The overall calculations required would embrace a variety of factors (see Table 8.6) and may thus prove to be contentious. It is not simply a question of the immediate impact of transhipment on freight transport but also that reduced numbers of goods vehicles on roads lead to the potential for more car traffic. Indeed, there was something of a stream of empirical studies on the subject of transhipment and consolidation of freight in the 1970s which, in terms of hard results, really produced very little (Button and Pearman, 1981). Consequently, while there may be a second-best case for forcing users to consolidate their consignments more than they do now (which in turn may well mean less JIT management in some countries) it seems improbable that it would do little more than move L_s somewhat closer to L_p.

8.9 Information and Attitudes

One final policy approach, and one which tends to be rather neglected in the mainstream of economics, is that of information and attitudes. Individuals' demands for any commodity are shifted by a change in 'tastes'. In practice, this catch-all variable has been thrown into the analysis quite simply to encapsulate those effects which economists cannot explain by more easily measured factors such as changes in income or the price of other commodities. In fact, social attitudes and the degree to which individuals have information about any product can influence sales quite significantly in some circumstances (Viek and Michon, 1991). At the most basic level one can point to the expenditure of large firms on advertising and marketing as they seek to push the demand curve for their product to the right. Certainly politicians seem to think it important, given the numerous statements and agreements which have been reached in recent meetings recognising the importance of changing peoples' attitudes towards such things as conservation.

The importance of information in the transport and environment context is that policies can, and in most countries have, been used to alter the travel habits of individuals and firms. At one level, there are the straightforward campaigns for environmental improvements of which those regarding safety are the most obvious (e.g. anti-drink-and-drive campaigns). Perhaps more subtly, designs of maps and sign posts, combined with radio travel bulletins are used to influence car and lorry traffic. In many cases such things are used explicitly to direct traffic away from environmentally sensitive urban areas. This is not simply a case of neutral information dissemination; the information is quiet clearly 'released' in such a way as to bias transport users' behaviour - increasing demand on some routes and reducing it on others. At another level, legislation has in many countries forced vehicle manufacturers to release, in a consistent and specified manner, details of such things as fuel consumption. This gives potential purchasers additional information upon which to base their final selection.

How powerful these individual initiatives are and whether they have enduring properties is difficult to say. Certainly there is considerable inertia in travel behaviour and this is difficult to overcome (Banister, 1978). But there is a further, and very much wider, dimension to this issue. This is the information which is more widely available to society and the impact that this has on consumption behaviour. There is evidence from opinion polls that there has been a trend towards greater awareness of environmental issues, although this does wax and wane a little as other, especially economic or security, matters come to the fore, and that this, in turn has begun to influence people's attitudes. To what extent this extends to the transport sphere it is difficult to say, in part because of explicit policies such as differential taxation for environmentally preferred fuels, additional safety regulations, new emissions standards for vehicles, etc.

Political Economy of Policy

9.1   Introduction

In this chapter we are concerned not so much with what policies are available to those trying to limit the adverse environmental impacts of transport, nor, are we so concerned with the implications of such policies on transport but rather we address the question of why in practice particular policy measures and packages are favoured by policy makers. What should be clear from what has gone before is that the current reality differs very considerably from the type of situation which many theoretical economists have tended to advocate in recent years. In particular, the employment of fiscal instruments to contain, even if not to optimise the environmental costs of transport, has been relatively limited. Examples have been cited (e.g. differential taxation for leaded fuel) but they are few and far between. Strictly the situation is not static and recent publications, for example by bodies such as the Organisation for Economic Cooperation and Development (1991b), indicate a gradual appreciation of the merits of such instruments. At the national level, the Dutch national environmental plan includes a consideration of financial instruments (Rietveld, 1992a).

Of course there are many circumstances where non-fiscal approaches are very logical and demonstrably more efficient, but whichever way one looks at it the usefulness of fiscal measures where they are appropriate is only slowly gaining in acceptance. Further, in many instances where fiscal tools are used in transport this must to some extent be seen as a reflection of the failure of command-and-control tools in other spheres, concerning matters such as containing industrial pollution, rather than as a positive view of a transport environmental policy involving the widespread use of fiscal instruments. In fact, transport controls are still dominated by fairly long-established techniques involving physical regulation and the setting of standards.

Of course, in many cases, there is no disagreement between what economists advocate and the command-and-control policies that are actually adopted. Standards and rules are often optimal when transaction costs are high when contrasted with comparable fiscal measures. In other cases there may be second-best reasons for adopting fiscal tools which do not produce a marginal social cost outcome. Here we are not concerned with these issues but rather with cases where the conventional positive, economic approach to environmental problems in the transport field are not adopted for other reasons.

9.2   The Question of Efficiency

In practice, economists have a traditional proclivity to favour fiscal policy instruments when considering environmental policy initiatives, although in recent years the appreciation of combined instruments such as tradeable permits have modified the views of some. However, when we look at the policies actually favoured by those in power we find that such tools are seldom deployed even in non-transport spheres (Common, 1990; Frey *et al*, 1985). There is, in effect, a general tendency to ignore economic instruments in this context. It is interesting to speculate why this is so. However, our understanding of why particular forms of policy instruments are preferred by policy makers when confronting environmental problems is incomplete although some work has recently come to the fore in the field. Only a very small amount of this, however, has been directly in the field of transport-induced environmental damage and policy but there is little reason to suspect that the more general findings do not extend to our area of interest.

Pezzey (1988) advanced a number of reasons why Pigouvian taxes in particular are often opposed. One problem is that we usually have very poor knowledge of the exact form of the damage function that underlies every MEC curve. This leaves the question of charges open to legal discussion and debate. Indeed, there may well be fears that the figures could end up being manipulated, possibly by the authorities to generate additional revenue. While there is undoubted truth in this view, in practice similar policies in other areas (e.g. regarding taxation of alcohol and tobacco) have gone ahead with equally scant information. The real point is that optimal Pigouvian taxes would only ever be arrived at by chance; the objective in practice is to introduce taxes as close to the optimum as is possible.

Further, the technical explanation for the lack of employment of fiscal instruments in the past cannot be for reasons of information availability; after all without adequate information it is equally impossible to establish the level of the optimal emissions standard as it is the optimal tax or charge.

Recognition of the fact that information is scant, indeed, has increasingly led to policy makers pursuing satisficing objectives by aiming to achieve environmental levels that conform to the best knowledge they have and are, in a general sense, seen as satisfactory. The issue then becomes, as we saw in Section 8.2 of the previous chapter, the attainment of these targets in the most efficient way possible. Efficiency, however, can take many forms, especially if thought of in terms of social rather than simple financial efficiency. What we effectively have is a list of criteria which may be relevant in the selection of the instrument to be used.

Exactly what goes into the list is debatable, and the weights attached to elements of it almost impossible to generalise about, but in a much cited study Baumol and Oates (1979) have suggested that the following are of relevance:

(a) *Dependability*. How reliable is the approach in achieving its objectives? Are its workings fairly certain and automatic or does it depend on a number of unpredictable elements?

(b) *Permanence*. Is the programme likely to be effective only so long as it captures public interest, or can it be expected to endure even when other issues have seized the attention of the media and the public?

(c) *Adaptability to Economic Growth*. Is the programme flexible enough to adapt to normal expansion in economic activities and population growth, both of which tend to accentuate problems of environmental damage?

(d) *Equity*. Does the programme divide its financial burden among individuals and enterprises fairly?

(e) *Incentives for Maximum Effort*. Does the programme offer inducements to individuals or enterprises to minimise environmental damage, or does it encourage no more than barely acceptable behaviour?

(f) *Economy*. Does the programme achieve its results at relatively low cost to society, or does it waste resources?

(g) *Political Attractiveness*. Is the method likely to recommend itself to legislators and voters?

(h) *Minimal Interference with Private Decisions*. Does the method tell the individual or businessman exactly what to do, or does it offer the broadest scope of choices consistent with protection of the environment?

Strict notions of satisficing imply that minimum targets (sometimes explicit but sometimes not) are set by policy makers regarding these various objectives. Since, however, it is generally impossible to achieve all of these minimum objectives, a certain amount of prioritisation is inevitable. Common (1989) offers some interesting observations on the priorities and the weights different groups put on the items included in the Baumol/Oates list.

The first is with regard to the equity issue. Normally it is assumed that regulations placing the immediate burden of reducing pollution on the generator rather than on those who suffer its effects is more equitable - hence the 'polluter-pays-principle'. Whether this is true or not is seldom tested empirically but seems rather to be accepted as an act of faith. It, nevertheless, enjoys a high position in the satisficing which takes place.

Second, the list does not include the informational demands placed on the agency responsible for administering the chosen policy. Many economists, though, favour fiscal measures because they feel them to be more efficient in this respect.

Finally, there is the issue of economy. The efficiency with which any policy instrument could do its job would play a significant role in most economists' decision framework. Others, though, often seem to misunderstand economists' strong interest in this criteria. It is frequently seen, according to Baumol and Oates (1979), as a matter of 'money grubbing'. In fact given the demands on resources there are good reasons for conducting policy economically so that maximum resources are available to meet other social objectives.

9.3 Some Theories of Policy Making

Policies, or at least the policy-makers, are often prisoners of history. The concern about the environment and the subsequent policy response that we have witnessed in recent years has, to a considerable extent, grown out of public health laws. These laws, while aimed specifically at health matters, also considerably improved many aspects of the local environment through the imposition of standards and public direction of resources. It is, therefore, to be expected that regulators experienced in this type of approach are often reluctant to take up newer economic frameworks. In the longer term this idea has its limitations, however, in the broader context of economic change which has been taking place in recent years with liberalisation, regulatory reform and privatisation becoming common place. Nevertheless, the more general experiences of environmental policy formulation in the US and the favouring of tradeable permits over emissions charges does perhaps support a tendency for the adoption of instruments with an element of 'familiarity' about them when changes have to be made. There are perhaps more subtle and complete models which can help explain the situation.

The Public Choice School of economic thought argues that standard notions of economic efficiency need to be combined with political reality to fully appreciate why particular types of economic policies are actually adopted. Much of the early work in the environmental field focused on questions of the protection of rent by incumbents and was akin to the debate about regulatory capture. Buchanan and Tullock (1975) in their seminal work, for instance, argue that direct regulations are preferred because they can act as a barrier to entry and hence to higher polluter profits for the incumbents. They conclude that 'observed quotas reflect the political power of regulatees'. Put another way, those groups which are meant to be controlled in fact capture the system (Posner, 1974; Peltzman, 1976). Bohm and Russell (1985) have also observed that firms can often prolong negotiations over the form and phasing in of command and control instruments and that delays their impact.

Scope for such rent-seeking activities in transport, because of such things as modal competition, is perhaps somewhat less than in some other fields where there is more scope for the exercise of monopoly or monopsony power. One can cite, perhaps, the case of night-time landing and take-off restrictions imposed for noise abatement purposes acting to secure the position of existing airports. Equally, high minimum technical legal requirements for vehicles imposed for safety and emission purposes can act to keep new manufacturers from the market or to deter foreign suppliers from attempting to penetrate it (e.g. European and US car manufacturers regularly accused the Japanese of such actions in the 1980s). In all of the cases where capture could occur one can perhaps add another reason to that of 'political power' indicated by Buchanan and Tullock. This additional reason is the ability of these large transport supplying concerns and vehicle manufacturers to control information flows. They generally have greater knowledge of the relevant technologies and possibilities and thus are inevitably influential in shaping the form of policies ultimately adopted by the authorities.

The strength of these arguments is, however, perhaps weaker in the transport field than in some other areas not only because of limitations in monopoly power but also because it is possible to cite counter examples where incumbents actually resist new environmental regulations (Rietveld, 1992b). The Dutch road haulage sector, for instance, strongly opposes regulatory measures designed to divert traffic to rail or inland waterways and prefers taxation measures within a market context if polluter-pays-policies are adopted (Bos, 1990).

The Buchanan/Tullock approach really fits into a much wider picture. This wider view takes into account the fact that those responsible for policy may have their own agenda (Stigler, 1971). The issue is often not one simply of the form of legislation adopted but also the *de facto* way in which regulators interpret and enforce the laws and codes for which they have responsibility. Again transport regulations do not seem to have been directly examined in any detail in this respect but there is a limited amount of information emerging from other areas of environmental policy. Work on establishing the 'Best Available Technology Economically Achievable' water control regulations in the US indicates that economic efficiency criteria, while strongly applied at the outset, diminished in importance over time. The conclusion was:

> Of course, this pattern (i.e. initial cost effectiveness then 'reasonable' control requirements) likely reflects the attitudes and decision making of personnel within the Agency during the tenure of these administrators, rather than the explicit decisions of the respective administrators. (Fraas and Munley, 1989)

The interesting question then, if one accepts this view, is one of what actually motivates policy makers. Recently a number of people have argued that policy makers take particular account of the distribution implications of alternative actions together with narrower posi-

tive questions of efficiency which academic economists tend to focus
on. This view takes into account the fact that, in democracies, the elec-
torate represents diverse groupings and the impacts on various income groups, in particular, of different policy options vary considerably (Hinich, 1991). This view is considered in some detail, in his
broad study of environmental policy, by Common (1989).

As we have seen above when considering Baumol and Oates' list,
the question of equity plays an important part in influencing the type
of transport policy adopted. It is worthwhile spending a little time
looking at the issues involved, especially with regard to the willingness of policy makers to trade-off efficiency for equity considerations.
Indeed, Common (1989) suggests:

> .... the general hypothesis that in choosing between instruments of pollution
> control democratic legislators give more weight to their perceptions of the
> various distributional implications than to efficiency criteria.

Whether this automatically leads to policy makers favouring
command-and-control instruments is not altogether clear. Some factors, however, seem to favour this view. One of the oft-stated advantages of charges over regulations is that they generate revenue which
can be used for redistributive purposes. In any sense equity concerns
can be addressed directly by means of appropriate transfer payments.
Indeed, the very collection of charges takes resources away from one
group and, irrespective of the benefits other groups may enjoy (e.g.
more peace and quiet, less risk of cancer, etc.) puts them in the hands
of government. Road pricing of congestion offers the simplest
illustration of this because we are concerned with the benefits and
costs to only two groups - motorists and government.

The standard diagram used in Chapter 7 is reintroduced (Figure
9.1). The optimal road price (RP) will yield revenue of ePad for the authorities - the immediate 'gainers' from the exercise. It is interesting to
see what happens to road users. Those who have been priced off the
road (i.e. Q*Q) will suffer a loss of consumer surplus of abc. Those who
remain (OQ*) now find they are paying P* per trip rather than P and
thus suffer an aggregate welfare loss of PP*ac. While simple arithmetic
shows a net social benefit when all parties are taken into account it is
clear that motorists as a group lose. (In fact there may be some high-in-
come motorists who remain on the road who benefit because they at-
tach extremely high values to travel-time savings but these are more
than cancelled out by those with lower valuations.)

The authorities could always redistribute the revenues to compensate losers and mitigate any perceived adverse distributional effects of
the policy. The difficulty, according to people such as Small (1992) and
Goodwin (1990), is to devise a technically sensible and politically acceptable mechanism for achieving this. Both authors, and others such
as Burtraw (1991) in the more general context of pollution charges,
come up with their own schemes but these are suggestive rather than

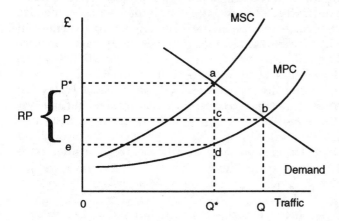

Figure 9.1
The revenue wedge

definitive. It could well be, therefore, that as much as to avoid the problems of spending revenue as for any other reasons emissions charges are avoided by policy makers.

Moving back one step, an interesting extension to this argument is the question of where exactly do regulators get their priorities from be it income distributional consequences or whatever. The Chicago School would argue that regulators are rational economic people who essentially favour and pursue policies which are to their own best interest. What this may mean depends on the details of the relevant institutional framework but, in general, one might think in terms of employment security, career prospects, good remuneration, etc. These types of goal can normally be more easily attained in a larger rather than smaller and in a more rather than less complex bureaucracy. Security is also achieved in a democracy by appealing to the largest possible constituency - hence the preoccupation found with the distribution implications of policy.

This notion of self-interest can be extended somewhat if we consider the existence of different coalitions of parties. After all while the bureaucrats may act to further their position other parties also have an interest in ensuring their objectives are achieved. Since compromise is almost inevitable, and recognised to be so, there are often good reasons for those involved to seek coalitions with other parties with similar goals. Outside of the environmental field, Keeler (1984) has developed this line of argument to explain changes in aviation, telecommunications and railroad regulations in the USA but little attempt seems to have been made to look at environmental policy in this way. One can easily envisage situations where particular groups combine to advocate specific policy measures.

Whether the notion of a coalition of interests would favour regulations over charges is difficult to say. What the studies cited above do indicate, though, is that there may be good reasons for suspecting that they might. The Buchanan/Tullock model implies that in many cases incumbent suppliers of transport services and hardware are likely to favour command-and-control approaches but really rather more is required to explain how their position is translated into policy. If, however, as Common and others argue, the policy makers themselves dislike fiscal instruments then a natural, and powerful coalition of interests emerges.

At a somewhat different level, and moving away from matters of direct self-interest, there are arguments that administrators favour regulatory controls for somewhat more ideological reasons. The line of argument here is that in some countries there is a general mistrust of market mechanisms which permeates all forms of public policy and, in consequence, a preference for regulatory approaches unless market-based approaches are demonstrably more attractive. Countries which adhere to the *Code Napoleon* form of legal structure are often seen as falling into this category. This contrasts to what is sometimes called the Anglo-Saxon approach where the market is favoured unless there are severe imperfections which can most effectively be tackled by direct intervention. Of course, we are talking in relative terms here but if the hypothesis holds it should be possible to examine the differing attitudes of regulators in countries which fall within each category. Frey *et al* (1985) did this by questioning economists employed as environmental civil servants and academics in a number of European states, and by drawing on the findings of similar work conducted in the US. The conclusion of the work is:

> It turns out that economists employed in a university, being theoretically inclined, with an ideology based to the right, and living in a market-oriented country such as Germany, Switzerland or the United States, *ceteris paribus* prefer the use of an effluent tax to individual prescriptions of emission levels. On the other hand, economists working in the public sector, with an ideology to the left, and living in a country with a long tradition of government intervention, such as Austria or France, *ceteris paribus* prefer a regulatory approach in environmental policy.

To what extent one can apply these findings in the transport field is uncertain although a cursory glance though the academic literature certainly finds support for the deployment of fiscal tools to tackle many transport-related environmental problems.

9.4   The International Dimension

Moving away from the general issue of motivation in environmental policy making we turn our attention briefly to the specific topic of international matters. As we have seen, it has become widely accepted that many of the adverse environmental consequences of modern society transcend national boundaries. This has led to an increased internationalisation of environmental policy making in recent years with a series of major high-level political meetings taking place around the World, the Rio meeting being the latest and most pronounced manifestation of the trend. It would be wrong to say that transport was the focal point of this internationalisation - it has not been. Transport is important, however, as a component of the wider debate if for no other reason than, as we saw in Chapter 3, that it is a significant contributor both to many trans-boundary and global environmental problems.

The difficulty in handling international environmental problems is essentially the lack of a clear incentive for any particular country to act alone (Barrett, 1991). The problem can be seen by considering the issue of global warming and the use of fossil fuels. In Figure 9.2 we depict, as is normal, the global marginal benefit of abatement as declining as abatement takes pace. The benefit to any individual country from acting unilaterally, however, will be considerably less than this - much of the gain from reduced global warming going to others. It does, however, have to bear the marginal costs of its actions which are likely to rise the more it modifies its activities. The logical action for the individual country is, thus, to reduce carbon emissions to a level Q^* which equates its own marginal costs with its own marginal benefits from abatement. Ideally, of course, global optimisation would require abatement to a level Q^t.

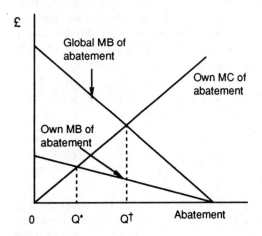

Figure 9.2
The divergence between national and global interests

The difficulty for international policy makers is to devise a structure which leads to attainment of Q^t. In fact, if all other countries co-operate and adopt policies which lead to local abatement equivalent to their Q^t then there is an incentive for remaining countries to follow suit. The reason behind this is that, while each country's costs of abatement exceed the non-co-operative benefits from abatement, the fact that everyone else is abating above their non-co-operative level makes all countries better off. Co-operation makes all parties better off. The problem is that of the free-rider. There are inevitable pressures for any member of the co-operative to reduce abatement levels quite simply because it will take account of savings in its own abatement costs but not of the social losses of imposing pollution on others.

There are several difficulties in reaching fully efficient agreements between individual countries. First, countries have differing cost and benefit curves which makes for divergence in the obligations they must bear and with imperfect information dispute is often the outcome. On the normative side there are also varying views, especially between the industrialised and Third World countries, as to what constitutes a 'just' obligation on their part. What this means in practice is that complex negotiations and sophisticated approaches to international environmental problems often give way to rather simple agreements. These represent compromise and can seldom be called efficient. They come about, according to Schelling (1960) because, 'the rationale may not be strong at the arbitrary "focal point", but at least it can defend itself with the argument "If not here, where?"'.

At the institutional level there are arguments, therefore, that the setting and enforcement of international limits should be taken out of the hands of national governments and be given over to an international body. Heber (1991), for instance, advocates such a move arguing that this is consistent with the idea of global property rights. In theory an international body is more likely to arrive at an efficient set of policies but in practice it is doubtful whether, given the pressures of lobbying groups, etc., this would actually materialise. There are also problems of enforcement; most international bodies which do exist have limited power of policing and even less of punishment.

References

Alexandre, A., Barde, J-Ph. and Pearce, D.W. (1980), 'The practical determination of a charge for noise pollution', *Journal of Transport Economics and Policy*, 14, 205-220.

Altshuler, A. and Teal, R. (1979), 'The political economy of airline deregulation', in Altshuler, A (ed), *Current Issues in Transportation Policy*, Lexington: Lexington Books.

Altshuler, A., Anderson, M., Jones, D., Roos, D. and Womack, J. (1984), *The Future of the Automobile*, Cambridge: MIT Press.

Andersen, B. (1992), 'Factors affecting European privatization and deregulation policies in local public transport: the evidence from Scandinavia', *Transportation Research*, 26A, 179-91.

Appleyard, D. (1981), *Livable Street*, Berkeley: University of California Press.

Ashworth, M. and Dilnot, A. (1987), 'Company car taxation', *Fiscal Studies*, 8, 24-38.

Banister, D. (1978), 'The influence of habit formation on model choice - a heuristic model', *Transportation*, 7, 5-19.

Barde, J-Ph. and Button, K.J. (eds) (1990), *Transport Policy and the Environment: Six Case Studies*, London: Earthscan.

Barrett, S. (1991), 'Economic analysis of international environmental agreements: lessons for a global warming treaty', in Organisation for Economic Cooperation and Development, *Responding to Climate Change: Selected Economic Issues*, Paris: OECD.

Baumol, W.J. and Oates, W.E. (1979), *Economics, Environmental Policy and the Quality of Life*, Englewood Cliffs: Prentice-Hall.

Baumol, W.J. and Oates, W.E. (1988), *The Theory of Environmental Policy*, Cambridge: Cambridge University Press.

Beckenham, A.F. (1985), 'Transport and nation-state governments world-wide: a further review', *Transport Reviews*, 5, 67-74.

Beesley, M.E. (1964), 'Technical possibilities of special taxation in relation to congestion caused by private cars', in European Conference of Ministers of Transport, *2nd International Symposium on Theory and Practice of Transport Economics*, Paris: ECMT.

Behbehani, R., Pendakur, V.S. and Armstrong Wright, A.T.(1984), *Singapore Area Licensing Scheme: A Review of the Impact*, Washington: World Bank Water Supply and Urban Development Department.

Blum, W. and Rothengatter, W. (1990), 'Case study of the Federal Republic of Germany', in Barde, J-P. and Button, K.J. (eds), *Transport Policy and the Environment: Six Case Studies*, London: Earthscan.

Boghani, A.B., Kimble, E.W. and Spencer, E.E. (1991), *Can Telecommunications Help Solve America's Transport Problems?*, Cambridge, Mass: Arthur D. Little.

Bohm, P. and Russell, C.S. (1985), 'Alternative policy instruments', in Kneese, A.V. (ed), *Handbook of Natural Resource and Energy Economics (Vol. 1)*, Amsterdam: North Holland.

Bos, M. (1990), 'Wegvervoer en Milieu, *Tijdschift voor Vervoerwtenschap*, 26, 40-52.

Bouladon, G. (1979), 'Costs and benefits of motor vehicles', in *Urban Transport and the Environment*, Seminar organised by the OECD and the ECMT: Paris.

Boulding, K. (1966), 'The economics of the coming spaceship Earth', in Jarret, H., (ed), *Environmental Quality in a Growing Economy*, Baltimore: Johns Hopkins University Press.

Boyle, K.J. and Bishop, R.C. (1985), 'The total value of wildlife resources: conceptual and empirical issues', paper presented to the Association of Environmental and Resource Economists Workshop on Recreational Demand Modelling, Boulder.

British Institute of Management Foundation (1979), *Business Cars: A Survey of Current Practice in 471 Organisations*, Management Survey Report No. 44, BIMF: London.

Buchanan, J. M. and Stubblebine, W. (1962), 'Externality', *Economica*, 29, 371-84.

Buchanan, J.M. and Tullock, G. (1975), 'Polluters profits and political response. Direct controls versus taxes', *American Economic Review*, 65, 39-47.

Burtraw, D. (1991), 'Compensating losers when cost-effective environmental policies are adopted', *Resources*, 104, 1-5.

Button, K.J. (1984), 'Road pricing - an outsider's view of American experiences', *Transport Reviews*, 4, 73-98.

Button, K.J. (1990a), 'Environmental externalities and transport policy', *Oxford Review of Economic Policy*, 6, 61-75.

Button, K.J. (1990a), 'Infrastructure plans for Europe', in Gillund, J. and Tornqvist, G.(eds), *European Networks*, Umea: CERUM.

Button, K.J. (1991a), 'The development of East-West European transport in the 1990s', in *Evolution in Transportation*, Quebec: CTRF.

Button, K.J. (1991b), 'Transport and communications', in Rickard, J.H. and Larkinson, J. (eds), *Long Term Transport Issues*, Aldershot: Avebury.

Button, K.J. (1992a), 'Privatization in the transport sector: some of the key issues', *Economisch en Sociaal Tijdschrift*, 45, 29-48.

Button, K.J. (1992b), 'The liberalisation of transport services', in Swann, D. (ed), *1992 and Beyond*, London: Routledge.

Button, K.J. (1992c), 'Transport regulation and the environment in low income countries', *Utilities Policy*, 2, 248-57.

Button, K.J. and Gillingwater, D. (1986), *Future Transport Policy*, London: Routledge.

Button, K.J. and Lauder, D. (1991), *Videoconferencing*, London: Department of Trade and Industry.

Button, K.J. and Ngoe, N. (1991), *Vehicle Ownership and Use Forecasting in Low Income Countries*, Transport and Road Research Laboratory Contractor Report 278: Crowthorne.

Button, K.J. and Pearce, D.W. (1989), 'Improving the urban environment: how to adjust national and local government policy instruments for sustainable urban growth', *Environment and Planning*, 30, 135-84.

Button, K.J. and Pearman, A.D. (1981), *The Economics of Urban Freight Transport*, London: Macmillan.

Button, K.J. and Rothengatter, W. (1992), 'Transport's contribution to global environmental pollution', in Banister, D. and Button, K.J. (eds), *Environmental Policy and Transport*, Spon's: London.

Button, K.J., Fowkes, A.S. and Pearman, A.D. (1982), *Car Ownership Modelling and Forecasting*, Aldershot: Gower Press.

Button, K.J., Pearman, A.D. and Fowkes, A.S. (1980), 'Car availability and public transport', *Rivista Internazionale di Economia dei Transporti*, 7, 339-43.

Cabajo, J. (1991), 'Accident and air pollution externalities in a system of road user charges', Informal Working Paper, Washington: World Bank.

Cameron, M. (1991), *Transportation Efficiency: tackling Southern California's Air Pollution and Congestion*, Los Angeles: Environmental Defense Fund and Regional Institute of Southern California

Cheslow, M.D. (1978), 'A preliminary analysis of a road pricing and transit improvement program in Berkeley, California', Urban Institute Paper, 5050-3-6: Washington.

Coase, R.H. (1960), 'The Problem of Social Cost', *Journal of Law and Economics*, 3,1-44.

Commission of the European Communities (1992a), *Towards Sustainability*, COM (92) 23 FINAL, EC: Brussels.

Commission of the European Communities (1992b), *A Community Strategy for 'Sustainable Mobility'*, COM (92), 46 FINAL, EC: Brussels.

Commission on the Third London Airport (1971), *Report*, London: HMSO.

Common, M.S. (1990), 'The choice of pollution control instruments: why is so little notice taken of economists' recommendations?', *Environment and Planning A*, 21,1297-314.

Crandall, R.W., Gruenspecht, H.K., Keeler, T.E. and Lave, L.B. (1986), *Regulating the Automobile*, Washington: Brookings Institution.

Cropper, M.L. and Oates, W.E. (1992), 'Environmental economics: a survey', *Journal of Economic Literature*, 30, 675-740.

Dawson, J.A.L. and Catling, I. (1986), 'Electronic road pricing in Hong Kong', *Transportation Research*, 20A, 129-34.

Deakin, E. (1990), 'Case study of the United States', in Barde, J-P. and Button, K.J. (eds), *Transport Policy and the Environment: Six Case Studies*, London: Earthscan.

DeMeza, D. and Gould, J.R. (1987), 'Free access versus private property in a resource: income distributions compared', *Journal of Political Economy*, 95, 1317-25.

Dewees, D.N. (1978), 'Estimating the time costs of highway congestion', *Econometrica*, 47, 1499-512.

Dickie, M. and Gerking, S. (1991), 'Willingness to pay for ozone control: inferences from the demand for medical care', *Journal of Environmental Economics and Management*, 21, 1-16.

Douglas, G. and Miller, J. (1974), *Economic Regulation of Domestic Air Transport: Theory and Policy*, Washington: Brookings Institution.

Drucker, P. (1990), 'The emerging theory of manufacturing', *Harvard Business Review*, 68: 97-102.

Elliott, W.E.Y. (1975), 'The Los Angeles affliction: some suggestions for a cure', *Public Interest*, 23,119-28.

European Conference of Ministers of Transport (1983), *Transport and Telecommunications*, Paris: ECMT.

European Conference of Ministers of Transport (1988), *Statistical Trends in Transport 1965-85*, Paris: ECMT.

Evans, A. W. (1992), 'Road congestion: the diagrammatic analysis', *Journal of Political Economy*, 100, 211-17.

Faiz, A., Sinha, K., Walsh, M. and Varma, A. (1990), 'Automotive air pollution: issues and options for developing countries', WPS 492, PRE Working Paper, World Bank, Washington.

Fisher, A.C. and Peterson, F.M. (1976), 'The environment in economics: a survey', *Journal of Economic Literature*, 14, 1-33

Foster, C.D. (1974), 'Transport and the urban environment', in Heggie, I.G. (ed) *Transport and the Urban Environment*, London: Macmillan.

Fraas, A.G. and Munley, V.G. (1989), 'Economic objectives with a bureaucratic decision process. Setting pollution control requirements under the Clean Act', *Journal of Environmental Economics and Management*, 17, 35-53.

Freeman, A.M. (1984), 'Depletable externalities and Pigouvian taxation', *Journal of Environmental Economics and Management*, 11, 173-9.

Frenking, H. (1988), *Exchange of Information on Noise Abatement Policies. Case Study on Germany*, Report Prepared for the Environmental Directorate of the OECD: Paris.

Frey, B.S., Schneider, F. and Pommerehne, W.W. (1985), 'Economists' opinions on environmental policy instruments: analysis of a survey', *Journal of Environmental Economics and Management*, 12, 62-71.

Friedlaender, A.F. (1981), 'Price distortions and second best investment rules in the transportation industries', *American Economic Review, Papers and Proceedings*, 71, 389-93.

Garrison, W.L. and Deakin, E. (1988), 'Travel, work and telecommunications: a view of the electronics revolution and its potential impact', *Transportation Research*, 22A, 239-46.

Gillen, D.W. (1978), 'Parking policy, parking location decisions and the distribution of congestion', *Transportation*, 7, 69-85.

Glazer, A. and Niskanen, E. (1992), 'Parking fees and congestion', *Regional Science and Urban Economics*, 22, 123-32.

Goldstein, G.S. and Moses, L.N. (1975), 'Transport controls and the spatial structure of urban areas', *American Economic Review, Papers and Proceedings*, 65, 289-94.

Gomez-Ibanez, J.A. and Fauth, G.R. (1980), 'Downtown auto restraint policies: the costs and benefits for Boston', *Journal of Transport Economics and Policy*, 14, 133-53.

Goodwin, P.B. (1990), 'How to make road pricing popular', *Economic Affairs*, 10, 6-7.

Goodwin, P.B. (1992), 'A review of new demand elasticities with special reference to short and long run effects of price changes', *Journal of Transport Economics and Policy*, 26, 155-70.

Greater London Council (1974), *Supplementary Licensing*, London: GLC.

Group Transport 2000 Plus (1991), *Transport in a Fast Changing Europe* (No place of publication).

Gwilliam, K.M. and Allport, R.J. (1982), 'A medium term transport research strategy for the EEC: Part 1', *Transport Reviews*, 2, 305-316.

Hahn, R. and Hester, G. (1989), 'Economic prescriptions for environmental problems: how the patient followed the doctor's orders', *Journal of Economic Perspectives*, 3, 95-114.

Hanks, J.W. and Lomax, T.J. (1990), *Roadway Congestion in Major Urbanised Areas 1982-to 1988*, College Station: Texas Transportation Institute.

Heber, B.P. (1991), 'The economic case for an international law of the atmosphere', *Government and Policy*, 9, 417-29.

Hensher, D.A. (1991), 'Electronic toll collection', *Transportation Research*, 25A, 9-16.

Herald, W.S. (1977), *Auto Restricted Zones: Plans for Five Cities*. Report UMTA-VA-06-0042-78-32, Washington: US Department of Transportation.

Hillman, M., Henderson, I. and Whalley, A. (1976), *Transport Realities and Planning Policy*, London: Political and Economic Planning.

Himanen, V., Nijkamp, P. and Padjen, J. (1992), 'Environmental quality and transport policy in Europe', *Transportation Research*, 26A, 147-157.

Hinich, M.J. (1991), 'A spatial theoretical approach to environmental politics', in Kraan, D.J. and in't Veld, R.J., *Environmental Protection: Public or Private Choice*, Boston: Kluwer.

Horowitz, J. (1982), *Air Quality Analysis for Urban Transportation Planning*, Cambridge, Mass: MIT Press.

Hughes, P. (1990), *Transport and the Greenhouse Effect*, Energy and Environmental Research Unit, Open University, Milton Keynes.

Independent Commission on Transport (1975), *Changing Directions*, Coronet: London.

Indian Ministry of Surface Transport, Transport Research Division (1986), *Special Issue on Motor Vehicle Accidents in India*, Government of India: New Delhi.

Inter-American Development Bank (1982), *The Impact of Energy Costs on Transportation in Latin America*, IADB: Washington.

Johansson, P-O. (1987), *The Economic Theory and Measurement of Environmental Benefits*, Cambridge: Cambridge University Press.

Jones-Lee, M.W. (1990), 'The value of transport safety', *Oxford Review of Economic Policy*, 6, 39-60.

Jones-Lee, M.W., Hammerton, M. and Philips, P.R. (1985), 'The value of safety: results of a national sample survey', *Economic Journal*, 95, 49-72.

Kanafani, A. (1983), *The Social Costs of Road Transport: A Review of Road Traffic Noise, Air Pollution and Accidents*, OECD DOC. ENV/TE/84.3: Paris.

Kealy, M.J. and Bishop, R.C. (1986), 'Theoretical and empirical specification issues in travel cost demand studies', *American Journal of Agricultural Economics*, 68, 660-7.

Keeler, T.E. (1984), 'Theories of regulation and the deregulation movement', *Public Choice*, 44, 103-45

Keeler, T.E. and Small, K.A. (1977), 'Optimal peak-load pricing, investment, and service levels on urban expressways', *Journal of Political Economy*, 85, 1-25.

Khisty, C.J. and Kaftanski, P.J. (1986), 'The social costs of traffic congestion during peak pours', paper presented to the 66th Annual Meeting of the Transportation Research Board, Washington: TRB.

Knight, F. (1924), 'Some fallacies in the interpretation of social costs', *Quarterly Journal of Economics*, 38, 582-606.

Kraus, M., Mohring, H. and Pinfold, T. (1976), 'The welfare costs of non-optimum pricing and investment policies for freeway transportation', *American Economic Review*, 66, 532-547.

Kroes, E.P. and Sheldon, R.J. (1988), 'Stated preference methods: an introduction', *Journal of Transport Economics and Policy*, 22, 11-25.

Krutilla, J.A. (1967), 'Conservation reconsidered', *American Economic Review*, 57, 777-86.

Kunert, U. (1988), 'National policy towards cars: the Federal Republic of Germany', *Transport Reviews*, 8, 59-74.

Kuzmyak, J.R. and Schreffler, E.N. (1990), *Evaluation of Travel Demand Management (TDM) Measures to Relieve Congestion*, US Federal Highway Administration, Report No. FHWA-SA-90-005, Springfield: National Technical Information Service

Laikin, R.E., Chadwick, M.J. and Cooke, J.G. (1987), 'Energy-based emission inventories for modelling cost-effective SO_2 and NO_X abatement strategies in Europe', paper presented at the International Workshop on Methodologies for Air Pollution Emission Inventories, Paris.

Lamure, C. (1990), 'Environmental considerations in transport investment', in *Ministerial Session on Transport and the Environment; Background Reports*, Paris: ECMT & OECD.

Lamure, C. and Quinet, E. (1990), 'Case study of France', in Barde, J-P. and Button, K.J. (eds), *Transport Policy and the Environment: Six Case Studies*, London: Earthscan.

Larsen, O.I., (1988), 'The toll ring in Bergen Norway - the first year of operation', *Traffic Engineering and Control*, 22, 216-22.

Lehmacher, H. (1990), 'The coordinating of the UN/ECE: projects and programmes', paper resented to a seminar on, Developing a European Transport Infrastructure Network: The Case of Inland Transport, Brussels: Centre for European Policy Studies.

Linster, M. (1989), 'Background facts and figures', in *Ministerial Session on Transport and the Environment; Background Reports*, Paris: ECMT & OECD.

Liroff, R.A. (1986), *Reforming Air Pollution Regulation: The Toil and Trouble of EPB's Bubble*, Washington: Conservation Foundation.

Maggi, R. (1989), 'Towards an economic theory of barriers to communication', *Papers of the Regional Science Association*, 66, 131-41.

Maler, K.G. (1974), 'Environmental policies and the role of the economist in influencing public policy', in Heggie, I.G. (ed) *Transport and the Urban Environment*, London: Macmillan.

McConnell, V.D. and Straszheim, M. (1982), 'Auto pollution and congestion in an urban model: an analysis of alternative strategies', *Journal of Urban Economics*, 11, 11-31.

Meade, J.E. (1973), *The Theory of Economic Externalities*, Geneva: Insitut Universitaire de Hautes Etudes.

Mishan, E.J. (1967), *The Costs of Economic Growth*, Harmondsworth: Penguin.

Mitchell, R.C. and Carson, R.T. (1989), *Using Surveys to Value Public Goods: the Contingency Valuation Method*, Washington: Resources for the Future.

Mohring, H. (1979), 'The benefits of reserved bus lanes, mass transit subsidies and marginal cost pricing in alleviating traffic congestion', in Mieskowksi, P. and Straszheim, M. (eds), *Issues in Urban Economics*, Baltimore: Johns Hopkins University Press.

Mohring, H. (1989), 'The role of fuel taxes in controlling congestion', in *Transport Policy, Management and Technology Towards 2001*, Ventura: Western Periodicals Co.

Morrison, S.A. (1986), 'A survey of road pricing', *Transportation Research*, 20A, 87-97.

National Research Council (1991), *Tanker Spills: Prevention by Design*, Washington: • National Academy Press.

National Society for Clean Air (1989), *Pollution Glossary*, London: NSCA.

Netherlands Ministry of Transport and Public Works (1989), *Rekening Rijden: Road Pricing in the Netherlands*, The Hague: Ministry of Transport and Public Works.

Netherlands Organisation for Applied Scientific Research (1989), *De Invloed van Telecommunicatie op Vervoer; Gevolgen voor Energie en Millieu*, Appledoorn: TNO.

Newbery, D.M. (1988) 'Road user charges in Britain', *Economic Journal (Conference Papers)*, 90, 161-76.

Newbery, D.M. (1990), 'Pricing and congestion: economic principles relevant to road pricing', *Oxford Review of Economic Policy*, 6, 22-38.

Nijkamp, P. (1977), *Theory and Application of Environmental Economics*, Amsterdam: North Holland.

Nijkamp, P. and Salomon, I. (1989), 'Future spatial impacts of telecommunication', *Transportation Planning and Technology*, 13, 275-97.

Nijkamp, P., Vleugel, J.M. and van Gent, H.A. (1990), 'Case study of the Netherlands', in Barde, J-P. and Button, K.J. (eds), *Transport Policy and the Environment: Six Case Studies*, London: Earthscan.

Nilles, J.M. (1988), 'Traffic reduction by telecommuting: a status review and selected bibliography', *Transportation Research*, 22A, 301-17.

Nilles, J.M., Carlson, F.R., Gray, P. and Hanneman, G.J. (1976), *The Telecommunications-Transportation Trade-off: Options for Tomorrow*, New York: Wiley.

Nordhaus, W.D. (1991), 'To slow or not to slow: the economics of the greenhouse effect', *Economic Journal*, 101, 920-37.

Organisation for Economic Cooperation and Development (1975), *The Polluter Pays Principle*, Paris: OECD.

Organisation for Economic Cooperation and Development (1983), *Effects of Traffic and Roads on the Environment in Urban Areas*, Paris: OECD.

Organisation for Economic Cooperation and Development (1986), *Fighting Noise*, Paris: OECD.

Organisation for Economic Cooperation and Development (1987), *Toll Financing and Private Sector Involvement in Road Infrastructure Development*, Paris: OECD.

Organisation for Economic Cooperation and Development (1988a), *Transporting Hazardous Goods*, Paris: OECD.

Organisation for Economic Cooperation and Development (1988b), *Transport and the Environment*, Paris: OECD.

Organisation for Economic Cooperation and Development (1988c), *Cities and Transport*, Paris: OECD.

Organisation for Economic Cooperation and Development (1990), *Noise Abatement Policies for the 1990s*, DOC ENV(90)10 Paris.

Organisation for Economic Cooperation and Development (1991a), *Recommendation of the Council on the use of Economic Instruments in Environmental Policy*, Paris: OECD.

Organisation for Economic Cooperation and Development (1991b), *Environmental Policy: How to Apply Economic Instruments*, Paris: OECD.

Organisation for Economic Cooperation and Development (1991c), *Fighting Noise*, Paris: OECD.

Owen, W. (1987), *Transportation and World Development*, London: Hutchinson.

Panzar, J.C. (1983), 'Regulatory Theory and the US Airline Experience', *Journal of Institutional and Theoretical Economics*, 139, 490-505.

Pearce, D.W. and Markandya, A. (1989), *Environmental Policy Benefits: Monetary Valuations*, Paris: OECD.

Pearce, D.W., Barde, J.Ph., and Lambert, J. (1984), 'Estimating the cost of noise pollution in France', *AMBIO*, 8.

Pearce, D.W., Markandya, A. and Barbier, E.B. (1989), *Blueprint for a Green Economy*, London: Earthscan.

Pearce, D.W. and Turner, R.K. (1990), *Economics of Natural Resources and the Environment*, London: Harvester Wheatsheaf.

Pease, J. (1990), 'Can Oldridge take Cambridge to a "first" in restraint?', *Local Transport*, 41, 10-11.

Peltzman, S. (1976), 'Towards a more general theory of regulation', *Journal of Law and Economics*, 19, 211-40.

Perrow, C. (1984). *Normal Accidents: Living with High Risk Technologies*, New York: Basic Books.

Pezzey, J. (1988), 'Market mechanisms of pollution control: "polluter pays", economic and practical aspect', in Turner, R.K. (ed), *Sustainable Environmental Management: Principles and Practice*, London: Belhaven.

Pigou, A. (1920), *The Economics of Welfare*, London: Macmillan.

Ponti, M. and Vittadini, M.R. (1990), 'Case study of Italy', in Barde, J-P. and Button, K.J. (eds), *Transport Policy and the Environment: Six Case Studies*, London: Earthscan.

Poret, M. (1976), Information Economy, Ph.D. Thesis, Institute of Communications Research, Stanford University.

Posner, R.A. (1974), 'Theories of economic regulation', *Bell Journal of Economics*, 5, 335-58.

Prest, A.R. and Turvey, R, (1965), 'Cost-benefit analysis - a survey', *Economic Journal*, 75, 683-735.

Pucher, J.A.; Markstedt, A. and Hirschman, I. (1983), 'Impacts of subsidies on the costs of urban transport', *Journal of Transport Economics and Policy*, 17, 155-76.

Quinet, E. (1990), *The Social Costs of Land Transport*, Environment Monograph N° 32, Paris: OECD.

Quinet, E. (1991), 'Pour une définition de la notion de coût social de l'environnement', *Economie Appliquée*, 44, 67-77.

Ramjerdi, F. (1989), 'Evaluation of the combination of area licensing scheme and different public transport subsidies as policy measures in the Stockholm County', presented to the International Conference on Urban Environmental Improvement and Economic Development, Berlin: OECD/ Senate of Berlin.

Rietveld, P. (1992a), 'Transport policy and the environment: the case of the Netherlands', in Banister, D. and Button, K.J. (eds), *Environmental Policy and Transport*, Spon's: London.

Rietveld, P. (1992b), 'Transport policies and the environment: a public choice perspective', presented to the 4th World Conference on Transport Research, Lyon.

Ross, A. and Mwiraria, M. (1989), *Road Safety: Review of World Bank Experience*, World Bank: Washington.

Rothenberg, J. (1970), 'The economics of congestion and pollution: an integrated view', *American Economic Review, Papers and Proceedings*, 60, 114-21.

Rothengatter, W. (1989), 'Economic aspects', in *Ministerial Session on Transport and the Environment; Background Reports*, Paris: ECMT & OECD.

Roundtable of European Industrialists (1987), *Need for Renewing Transport Infrastructure in Europe - Prospects for Improving the Decision-making Process*, Brussels: ERI.

Salomon, I. (1984), 'Man and his transport behaviour. Part 1a. telecommuting - promises and reality', *Transport Reviews*, 4, 103-14.

Salomon, I. (1985), 'Telecommunications and travel: substitution or modified mobility', *Journal of Transport Economics and Policy*, 19, 219-35.

Salomon, I. (1988), 'Telecommunications and travel relationship: a review', *Transportation Research*, 20A, 223-38.

Sathaye, J. and Meyers, S. (1987), 'Transport and home energy use in cities of the developing countries: a review', *Energy Journal*, 8, 85-104.

Schelling, T.C. (1960), *The Strategy of Conflict*, Cambridge: Harvard University Press.

Schelling, T.C. (1992), 'Some economics of global warming', *American Economic Review*, 82, 1-14.

Schneider, L.M. (1985), 'New era in transportation strategy', *Harvard Business Review*, 63, 118-6.

Schultz, W. (1987), 'The economic costs of air pollution', paper presented to a seminar on The Future for Forests: London.

Seidenfus, H.St. (1990), 'Prospects for railways', in European Conference of Ministers of Transport, *Development Prospects for European Transport Between East and West*, Paris: ECMT.

Sharp, C.H. and Jennings, A. (1976), *Transport and the Environment*, Leicester: Leicester University Press.

Sherman, R. (1967), 'A private ownership bias in transit choice', *American Economic Review*, 57, 1211-7.

Small, K.A. (1992), 'Using the revenues from congestion pricing', paper presented to the Congestion Pricing Symposium, Arlington: Federal Transit Administration and Reason Foundation.

Small, K.A., Winston, C. and Evans, C.A. (1989), *Road Works - A New Highway Pricing and Investment Policy*, Washington: Brookings Institution.

Solheim, T. (1990), 'The toll-ring in Oslo', paper presented to the Ecology and Transport Conference, Gothenburg.

Spielberg, F. (1978), 'Transportation improvements in Madison, Wisconsin: preliminary analysis of pricing programs for roads and parking in conjunction with transit changes', Urban Institute Paper 5050-3-7: Washington.

Starkie, D.N.M. and Johnson, D.M. (1975), *The Economic Value of Peace and Quiet*, London: Saxon House.

Starrs, M.M. and Starkie, D.N.M. (1986), 'An integrated road pricing and investment model: a South Australian application', *Australian Road Research*, 16, 1-9.

Stigler, G.J. (1971), 'The theory of economic regulation', *Bell Journal of Economics*, 2, 3-21.

Theesuwes, J. (1991), 'Regulation or taxation', in Kraan, D.J. and in't Veld, R.J., *Environmental Protection: Public or Private Choice*, Boston: Kluwer.

Thompson, A. (1990), 'Road user charging - the current state of technology', *Traffic Engineering and Control*, 31, 526-32.

Thomson, J.M. (1974), *Modern Transport Economics*, Harmondsworth: Penguin.

Transnet (1990), *Energy, Transport and the Environment*, London: Transnet.

Tyler, M. (1979), 'Implications for transport', in *Impacts of Telecommunications on Planning and Transport*, Department of the Environment and Transport Research Report, No. 24, London

UK Department of Transport (1978), *Report of the Advisory Committee on Truck Road Assessment*, London: HMSO.

UK Department of Transport (1989a), *COBA 9 Manual*, London: Department of Transport.

UK Department of Transport (1989b), *The Allocation of Road Track Costs 1989/90*, London: Department of Transport.

UK Department of Transport (1989c), *Roads for Prosperity*, Cm 693, London: HMSO.

UK Department of Transport (1992), *Assessing the Environmental Impact of Road Schemes*, London: HMSO.

UK House of Commons Committee of Public Accounts, (1989), *Fifteenth Report - Road Planning*, HC 101, London: HMSO.

UK Ministry of Transport (1963), *Traffic in Towns*, London: HMSO.

UK Ministry of Transport (1964), *Road Pricing: The Economic and Technical Possibilities*, London: HMSO.

UK Office of the Ministry of Science (1963), *Noise, Final Report of the Committee on the Problem of Noise*, Cmnd 2056, London: HMSO.

United Nations (1990), *World Population Prospects*, New York: UN.

United Nations Economic Commission for Europe (1987), 'Consumption patterns in the ECE region: long-term trends and policy issues', *Economic Bulletin For Europe*, 39, 245-482.

US Congress, Office of Technology Assessment (1986), *Transportation of Hazardous Materials*, OTA-SET-304, Washington: US Government Printing Office.

US National Highway Traffic Safety Administration (1983), *The Economic Costs to Society of Motor Vehicle Accidents*, Department of Transportation HS-806-342: Washington.

van Huut, H. (1991), 'The right business in the right place', in *Proceedings of Seminar A*, London: PTRC Summer Meeting.

Vickrey, W. S. (1963), 'Pricing in urban and suburban transport', *American Economic Review, Papers and Proceedings*, 53, 452-65.

Viek, C. and Michon, J.A. (1991), 'Why we should and how we could decrease the use of motor vehicles in the near future', presented to the International Scientific Initiatives on Road Traffic Second Roundtable, Stockholm..

Viton, P.A. (1980), 'Equilibrium short-run marginal cost pricing of a transport facility: the case of the San Francisco Bay Bridge', *Journal of Transport Economics and Policy*, 14, 185-203.

Walters, A.A. (1961), *The Economics of Road User Charges*, Baltimore: Johns Hopkins University Press.

Webster, F.V. and Bly, P.H. (eds), (1980), *The Demand for Public Transport*, Report of the International Collaborative Study of the Factors Affecting Public Transport Patronage, Transport and Road Research Laboratory: Crowthorne.

Weitzman, M.L. (1974), 'Prices vs quantities', *Review of Economic Studies*, 41, 477-9.

Wheaton, W.C. (1978), 'Price-induced distortions in urban highway investment', *Bell Journal of Economics*, 9, 622-32.

Whiffen, A.C. and Leonard, D.R. (1971), *A Survey of Traffic Induced Vibrations*, Road Laboratory Report LR 418: Crowthorne.

Willson, R.W. and Shoup, D.C. (1990), 'Parking subsidies and travel choice: assessing the evidence', *Transportation*, 11, 141-57.

World Commission on Environment and Development (1987), *Our Common Future*, Oxford: Oxford University Press.

Zahavi, Y. (1979), *The "UMOT" Project*, US Department of Transportation Report DOT-RSPA-DPB-2-79-3: Washington.

Index